Happy *Even* After

Happy *Even* After

New Life after a Broken Relationship

PAT EDMISTON

WITH DAVID WAITE

FOREWORD BY

JENNIFER REES LARCOMBE

GRAND RAPIDS, MICHIGAN 49530

ZONDERVAN™

Happy Even After
Copyright © 2002 by Pat Edmiston with David Waite

Requests for information should be addressed to:
Zondervan, *Grand Rapids, Michigan 49530*

Pat Edmiston and David Waite assert the moral right to be identified as the authors of this work.

ISBN 0-007-13312-X

Interior design by Beth Shagene

Printed and bound in the United Kingdom

02 03 04 05 06 07 08 /❖OMN/ 10 9 8 7 6 5 4 3 2 1

*I would like to dedicate this book
to my three wonderful children
and their spouses, and my grandchildren
who are all such a blessing from the Lord.*

Contents

Acknowledgements

*P*utting down on paper numerous experiences from my life has proved to be an interesting and challenging task! It caused me to recall events and places that I had not thought about for many years, some amusing, some challenging and some that I now realize had a long-term impact on my life. Although it was necessary to try to remember details, places and circumstances, it was the friends I have made along the path of life who stood out most in my memories, and it is those dear folk I would especially like to acknowledge here. Some I have known since my schooldays, others have come into my life in more recent years, and there are those who seem to have been around – sent by God, I am sure – just at the times when I needed their support and friendship the most.

I would really love to mention by name all who supported me, prayed for me daily and challenged me to forgive as Christ forgave us, but even if my editor allowed me to be so indulgent, I would almost certainly unintentionally miss one or two from the list. I do not need to mention you all by name – you know who you are – and you will never fully realize just how much your sacrificial love and care helped me to come through this extremely difficult season of my life.

Many who come into that category are members of the church with which I have been associated since it began in 1975, and I would therefore like to thank the pastor, elders and members of the Bedworth Christian Centre for their love and care. I know that God will reward them in an abundant manner as His Word promises.

I would like to think that everyone is fortunate enough to have special God-given friends to enrich and brighten their lives. One such person whom I have been given is my dear friend Joy Davies, who helped me with the cleaning and domestic running of my household for many years. Joy certainly lived up to her name as she always filled my home with much laughter and mirth. This dear, Godly lady walked with me daily through my pain and I shall always be grateful to the Lord for bringing her into my life.

I would also like to acknowledge my good friends Ron and Pauline Harris. Pauline helps with my paperwork and makes sure my bills are all paid on time. Ron is a builder by trade and his expertise has been put to good use in the work of the Lord in this country and also in Zimbabwe. They both have a special ministry of encouragement and I know that God will reward them for their sacrificial care and support.

My thanks also go to my lifelong friend Lyn, whom I have known since my schooldays. As you will read in the pages of this book, she was, in a way, instrumental in getting Bob and me together in the first place. We in turn were able to introduce her to her husband, who attended the same school as Bob for a while. Lyn has stood by me through thick and thin and we have enjoyed each other's friendship for over 40 years, even though our lives took vastly different paths, causing us to live in different parts of the country for over 30 of those years.

Rob and Hilary Mackenzie have proved to be good, strong, reliable friends, who were always there for me, just as I tried to be there for them. Circumstances often seemed to occur that caused the Holy Spirit to bring us together, and frequently resulted in us laughing and crying together.

So, these are just a few of the friends whom God has so graciously put beside me and to whom I owe so much. But what about those whom I have failed to mention? Well, I know that God will reward each of you, which in the end will be far more precious than any reference I could have made in this book.

In addition to the good friends God has given me, I have also been especially blessed with three wonderful children, who become more precious to me each day. They have been a wonderful support to both Bob and myself, even though the marriage break-up was far from easy for any of them to bear. Children are surely a precious gift from God. They all live close by, so they are never very far away. Andrew and his wife Alison have given us four adorable granddaughters, Georgia, Kate, Beth and Ellie. As they grow, I pray that God will grant me the pleasure of sharing with them some of the truths He has taught me. Debbie, the artistic one in the family, married to Matt, has a unique sense of humour which has carried me through many sad times. Angela, married to Noel, has been blessed with a warm and friendly personality, and works as PA to our church pastors. There is a deep passion within them all to serve God, which is truly great to see. I am so blessed.

I also very much want to pay tribute to my sister-in-law, Viv, who proved to be such a valuable provider of support and encouragement. When I was unable to cope or think straight, she was a special source of comfort, even though she was also trying to come to terms with many painful issues herself. We would often chat together late into the night, her many words of reassurance and wisdom finding a permanent lodging place in my heart.

My thanks also go to David and Alison Waite for their daily prayers and support. Without them this book would never have been written. Also to Amy Boucher Pye, my commissioning editor, who had the faith to take on this project and has guided David and myself with great skill and expertise.

My final thanks go to all you readers for sparing the time, which is indeed so precious, to come with me through the pages of this book. My prayer is that you will come into a deeper relationship with the Lord and hunger after Him and His Word as never before, so that you are able to rise above anything that life sends, knowing that God is true to His Word and that He is without doubt able to do exceedingly abundantly above all that we can ask or think. Our faithful God will never let you down.

Foreword

by Jennifer Rees Larcombe

It must have taken Pat a great deal of courage to write this book. It is not easy to expose your heart to the scrutiny of the world, but it is so obvious that Pat's only motive in doing so is to share with others, struggling through their own nightmares, that God can be trusted. He really is there when everything else in life has broken into painful pieces. He can, and does, mend broken people and broken lives.

This is not just a book for people whose marriages have failed. Pat wisely gives advice and sensible warnings for people who are going through difficulties, and who may be allowing themselves to drift into danger. Her exploration of the difference between a peacemaker and a peacekeeper is masterly. On occasions love has to be brave enough to confront the situations most of us prefer to ignore, but we do so at our peril. For me, one of the greatest treasures of this book is Pat's clear message to us all that we are not responsible for other people, but we *are* responsible for our own attitudes, responses and reactions. We cannot change others, but we can change ourselves – with God's help.

I have never met Pat Edmiston, but by the time I had finished reading her book I felt so close to her I could have been her identical twin sister! Our stories are so similar, it felt uncanny. Our marriages both lasted 30 years, were happy and produced children who grew up to know and follow the Lord. Our husbands were both men who served God with all their energy, were fine husbands and devoted fathers, respected elders in their churches and men of integrity in the world. We both had the same struggles over forgiveness, and we both felt like giving up, crawling into a hole and hiding our heads in shame. So many similarities! As I read Pat's book, compulsively throughout one night, I kept muttering, 'Yes! I felt like that. Yes! Me too!'

What is most striking of all is the way God has given us both a new and closer-than-ever relationship with Himself in our new circumstances. So many of the Bible verses which comforted Pat have become my 'lifelines' too. The Lord lifted us both up again from total despair, and gave us the job of helping and comforting others in His name.

This book, which is full of spiritual nuggets, will be a great encouragement to many people who, like me, will identify with Pat's story on many levels. It is well written, a thoroughly good read and totally honouring to God.

ONE

Reflections

With each downward step that I took in order to get to the swimming pool, built beneath the main living room in my house, I could feel my spirit sinking deeper too. I had been a Christian for many years and yet, at this moment, it seemed that God had abandoned me. I walked through the swimming pool doors, and saw the bright morning light which streamed through the picture window playing on the water, causing a thousand diamonds to dance on its surface. I stopped at the edge of the pool and, as I looked down to the pale blue bottom, the thought crossed my mind that there was one quick way out of all my immediate anguish and hurt. The thought was gone in a moment – it was too ridiculous to contemplate.

Instead of getting into the pool, I started to walk around it, time and time again, praying as I walked. That morning there was a far greater urgency within me to pray than to swim. I was just a day away from my divorce becoming absolute, after 30 years of marriage. Soon after my husband left, I felt that God had given me a promise straight from His Word. As I read the Bible one morning, the words seemed to jump out at me: 'No weapon that is formed against you shall prosper' (Isaiah 54:17 NKJV). It seemed at the time that God was saying through the verse that whatever happened to me or came against me could never possibly succeed and that He would be my protection and help if I fully trusted Him, even though I had made numerous blunders and mistakes. Now the verse I had hung onto for months seemed more like a sick joke. Divorce was a pretty good weapon, I reckoned, and it was just 24 hours away.

Thinking back on the past

There were so many emotions going round and round in my head as I cried out to God at the side of the pool. I had been married to Bob for three decades. When we first got to know each other we were both youngsters, and we were at that time far from wealthy. In fact, neither of us came from affluent backgrounds. Bob was working as a clerk, and I was a shorthand typist in London. After we married, however, our faith in God and Bob's business skills eventually made him into one of the richest men in Britain.

We were both committed Christians, and it had been a good marriage. Bob had been a good husband and devoted dad, taking a genuine interest in our children, providing a happy, stable home life and fun-filled holidays, both in this country and abroad, for all of us. Our three children had developed into well-adjusted adults, who loved and served God as much as we did. People used to remark what a close, loving family we were – and it was true. Trouble seldom knocked on our door.

We had bought the house in which I was now living in 1979, and had spent two dust-filled years extending it just a few years ago. Set in 14 acres of rolling countryside on the outskirts of Coventry, it was what many people could only dream of. Apart from the indoor pool, it had a full-size tennis court, eight bedrooms, and a wonderfully spacious living room. The house was always full of life, especially when the family were all together. It was a home that our children loved and still do today, although they are all married now and have homes of their own. It had a rich homeliness that was often remarked on by our many visitors.

I sat down on one of the chairs placed around the pool and tried to think back over the events of the last few years. Was there a point somewhere along the way where I had gone wrong, or had stopped hearing God? I needed to know for myself – but that was not the only reason. Too many of my friends were finding themselves in the same situation, and I needed to know why. All marriages go through difficult patches, but divorce was a completely different matter. Personalities were involved, but the problem obviously went deeper than that, and until I got some answers, I would not be able to help myself – or anyone else, for that matter.

Just like any other couple, it had taken a while for both of us to adjust to married life: two becoming one does not happen overnight! But we were both young and we loved each other dearly, and any small teething problems were quickly forgotten as we set about establishing a home together. We were both active in our local church, and we wanted to honour God in everything that we did. When our first child was on the way I gave up work to be a full-time mum, as most women did in those days if they were able to, and Bob did what he could to further his career, eventually becoming chairman of a highly successful company.

Both our daughters had married and left the family home in the same year. As they were our last two children to leave the nest, it created something of a void. Letting go of your children is a very unsettling and emotional experience which requires considerable adjustment. Angela was married in June 1996, and our eldest daughter Debbie just five months later. That had been an action-packed year for us both as we prepared for these special family occasions. We looked forward to the weddings with great anticipation, since relatives were travelling from all over the world to join in the celebrations.

Our son Andrew had married his wife Alison back in 1990, and by the time Bob left they had provided us with two lovely granddaughters.

Once our children were all married, we found ourselves in one of those periods that most marriages go through – a time of readjustment. It could have been a positive rather than a negative experience. After all the years of bringing up a family, which had presented us with many challenges and demanded many sacrifices, at last we had a chance to enjoy some of the fruits of our labour, be more independent and, at the same time, enjoy time together with our children and grandchildren. Yet here we were, just about to be divorced, in spite of the fact that between us we had 78 years of Christian life experience on which to draw – and both of us were the type to face problems rather than throw in the towel and admit defeat.

The Christmas of 1996 was a particularly difficult one. At the time I put it down to the fact that neither of us was looking forward to saying a further goodbye to our daughter Angela, who was due to go to Australia with her new husband for a year at the start of 1997 – but events proved otherwise. We were all due to go on a family skiing holiday to France after the Christmas celebrations, which is something we always did and which was greatly looked forward to each year. We usually all travelled to the Alps together a couple of days after the Christmas break, but this time Bob suddenly decided to leave on Boxing Day, taking Russell, a cousin of ours, as his only travelling companion. His actions seemed a bit unusual as it was the one day of the year when we normally relaxed and had fun together as a family.

Bob seemed very preoccupied and a little distant during the holiday. Then, as soon as Angela and her husband had left for Australia later that month, he told me that he had twice been to see a marriage counsellor, and he wanted me to go along with him when he went to his next appointment. This was the first that I knew of his need to seek outside help to sort out any problems he felt we might have in our marriage. I readily agreed to go along with him, very much wanting to restore our relationship and solve any difficulties, which I think took him by complete surprise. Looking back, I am sure he expected me to refuse flatly.

We had our first meeting with the marriage counsellor on 6 February 1997, and there was a further meeting a few weeks later. In a joint session he had with us on the second visit, the counsellor stated that he felt there was a lot of respect in the marriage and it stood an excellent chance of surviving. We never went back again after that second visit.

Then, on 2 May 1997, Bob left home very suddenly, without warning. It was the day after the Labour Party celebrated their General Election victory, and just the day before we had gone to the polling station together. He stayed away until 6 June, a date which also stuck in my mind because of another celebration remembered on that date – D-day. I was overjoyed when he returned and believed that we were now over the worst, and indeed things did look very hopeful as we planned a holiday together in Australia, to visit Bob's brother and our daughter Angela and her husband Noel.

During the holiday, however, Bob received several phone calls, from various people, which clearly seemed to upset him. Immediately our time in Australia was over, even though we had enjoyed a really lovely, relaxing time, he once again packed his bags and left – and did not return. After his somewhat hasty departure, he went straight to his lawyer, ringing me to say that I would shortly be receiving divorce papers. They arrived the next morning.

After that there was very little communication between us – except, of course, for the dreaded legal correspondence that began to arrive – partly because I did not know for some time where he was living, and neither did many other people, for that matter. In so many painful ways, 1997 was turning out to be a complete contrast to the happy events of the previous year.

Ripple effects of divorce

I knew that I could not change Bob's heart – that was up to God. Yet, with His help, I could certainly do something about mine. I therefore had to concentrate on my own attitude and response to the whole situation, and I suppose my feelings were typical of someone going through this set of circumstances, whether they have a faith in God or not.

I ran the whole gamut of emotions. Incredible pain, anger, rejection and hopelessness: they all came to mock me. I felt that my whole world was collapsing around me and that I could have worked a whole lot harder at saving my marriage. I found myself at one point beating the floor of my living room with my fists in sheer frustration at not being able to talk to Bob, or get through to him in any way. It seemed for a while that God had forsaken me, and it was as though there was a dark evil hanging over me, controlling our marriage and indeed the whole of my family.

The situation would have been far more understandable if we had been the type of couple who constantly argued and disagreed – but we rarely did. Looking back, maybe it would have been better if we had quarrelled more often. When I received the petition, the reasons for the divorce seemed to be very trivial, and none of the claims in the petition was strong enough grounds for divorce anyway. In fact, I am sure that everything could have been resolved if we had both really and truly wanted to do it. The Bible states that 'with God all things are possible' (Matthew 19:26) and I certainly believed that, even though with our natural mind things seem impossible, 'God can do exceedingly abundantly above all that we can ask or think, according to the power that works in us' (Ephesians 3:20).

Other people, especially at church, naturally started to notice that something was going on between us over the months. Nothing had yet been announced officially, as I wanted to protect others from the facts for as long as possible, hoping and praying that maybe all would be well and they would never need to know. Many questions were being asked by church members, however, and it became almost impossible to keep quiet any longer. Just before we left for Australia, in an effort to stop the various rumours that had started to circulate, it was agreed that a statement would be read to the church while we were both on holiday, saying in effect that we were having problems in our marriage, there was someone else involved who was also a member of our church, and we were working to resolve and overcome our difficulties. The whole church was saddened, of course, but also very sympathetic to the situation. They were then asked to support us by making the restoration of our marriage a special matter for prayer. As soon as we returned from our time in Australia, however, Bob left anyway.

This news was not passed on to anyone, since at that stage none of us knew whether the situation would change yet again. So when I went to church the following Sunday, people assured me that they were praying for us both and our future together – when in fact Bob had already filed for divorce. Going to church each Sunday during that period was one of the hardest things I had ever had to do. I tried to have my children and grandchildren around me as much as I could, as a sort of protection from people's enquiries, even though I knew they came from those who were genuinely concerned and sincerely cared about us both.

By this time we were attending a church in Bedworth which Bob and I had been instrumental in founding over 20 years earlier, and I am sure a lot of people did not really know what to make of it all, or how to handle the situation once they discovered that Bob had finally left. He was an elder and a well-respected member of the church, and folk often turned to him for his wise financial and spiritual advice. Suddenly he was no longer around, and it seemed at first to produce mixed emotions, and perhaps anger, within the Fellowship as people began to realize the serious implications that were involved.

It was then that I started to understand that divorce is not just about two people splitting up. Like the ripples in our swimming pool, such a decision impacts on an increasingly wider circle of people. Children, grandchildren, in-laws, friends, business contacts – the list goes on.

In time, the realization that Bob had finally left started to throw the church members onto God and His Word for answers. Eventually both the pastor and the church began to grow and mature spiritually as biblical truths became reality. We learned that we can be overcomers and live victorious lives in whatever circumstances we find ourselves, and that situations which the devil intends for bad, God can without a doubt turn around for good if we obey Him, choose to walk in His ways and handle trials and tribulations the way He instructs us to. They say that God is a great economist and never wastes anything given to Him, and it was certainly proving to be the case in this situation.

Meanwhile, my own family were in turmoil. Our separation and Bob's subsequent departure from the family home caused much heartache and tension all round, as each member was struggling to deal with his or her own hurts and damaged emotions. It emerged that Bob had spoken to each of our children at some point or other, indicating what he might do. Looking back, I would have been wiser to have talked to them about my fears for our marriage months and even years before, and to have asked them to pray for us – but I did not.

I was, I suppose, adopting a very passive attitude to the situation, hoping deep down that the problems might just go away, and that the family would therefore never need to know. That was not to be, however, and the situation just accelerated, without the protecting prayers of our children. Things were just starting to calm down when Angela and Noel returned from their year in Australia, and they too had to adjust themselves to the new situation, which in turn opened up the whole thing again with the rest of the family.

Message from God

I suddenly realized that I had been staring at the empty pool in a vacant sort of way for some time, reflecting on the events that had brought me to the point where I was now. I decided to swim a few lengths before climbing the stairs back to the ground floor of the house. I still could not get out of my mind the fact that I had felt God had given me the 'no weapon' scripture, and yet that was just what appeared to be happening. I wondered what the future would really hold for me now. Would I just become a grandma, knitting bootees and babysitting my grandchildren – wonderful as that was – or would God still be able to use me further in the new role in which I found myself?

Walking into the kitchen to make myself a cup of tea, I noticed that Benny Hinn's morning programme on the Christian Channel was in full swing. I had discovered this television channel some time before, and had been greatly helped and encouraged by the various speakers who taught biblical truth, relating it closely to everyday issues. The ministry of people like Joyce Meyer and T.D. Jakes, as well as Benny Hinn himself, had become such a tremendous blessing that I had started to tape the programmes, which began early in the morning, so that I could watch them at a more convenient time.

I took my cup of tea into the bedroom, where I had left the television broadcasting to the empty room. It too was tuned to the Christian Channel, and Benny Hinn was still speaking. Something he was saying made me stop and listen, even though I knew I could hear it later from the tape. So often I had half-listened to him praying for people with heart trouble, arthritis, or other painful conditions, but today I heard him saying that he felt God was speaking to someone, a lady. . . . He stopped and then said, 'Yes, it's definitely for a lady, who has gone through great trials, much sorrow and pain. God has not forgotten the call on your life. God has a plan and a purpose for you, and within two years it's all going to happen.' Then he prayed, 'Release that one. Bring that vision you have given them to fulfilment.'

I had watched Benny Hinn's programme so many times before, but as he spoke I somehow knew that God was using him to speak to me. The facts were that I had been keen to use what resources I had for the Lord. As I had gone through my own personal nightmare while my marriage fell apart, I began to be more and more aware of Christians, myself included, who were going through a whole range of situations that they did not understand and could not overcome, because they did not know how to apply the Word of God effectively, or how to become victors instead of victims.

I had mentioned to my pastor some time before that I had a growing desire to set up a foundation that would equip and train Christians to deal with these types of situations from a biblical standpoint, as well as spreading the good news of the gospel of Jesus Christ, not just in this country, but into the far corners of the earth as the Bible instructs us. I had even enquired about a building just down the road from where I lived, which had suddenly appeared on the market and would have been perfect as a base for such an undertaking, but I had been told a couple of months before that a bid had been accepted from a group outside the area.

So everything on that score had apparently come to a dead end. Yet I was now aware of a growing sense of excitement within me as I mulled over Benny Hinn's words: 'God has not forgotten the call on your life.' Could this be God's way of telling me that He would in some way resurrect the plans that I had in my heart? Or was that a completely forlorn hope? I was well aware that in certain sections of the Christian Church some people found it difficult to cope with the idea of women in any kind of ministry role. In the light of that, a divorced woman, even if she was considered to be the 'innocent' party, would be completely beyond the pale for many.

My thoughts were interrupted by the phone. On the line was Ralph Coleman, a family friend and a founder member of our church whom we had known since moving to the Midlands many years before. He was the church treasurer, and a well-respected member of the Fellowship. I had previously shared with him and my son Andrew my desire to set up a Christian foundation and ministry centre that would, ideally, be locally based. Knowing Ralph to be highly efficient and trustworthy, I had asked him to deal with the estate agents as far as a possible building was concerned, because I wanted to keep my name out of the frame at that point. As I mentioned, we had already pursued one building which would have been ideal, but had been told that it was sold and no longer on the market. Now, as Ralph started to speak, I could tell that he was excited about something.

'Pat, I'm sorry to ring you so early in the morning,' he said, sounding a little breathless, 'but I've just opened my morning post. There's a letter from the estate agents, saying that the building we were after is on the market again. What do you think about that?' Without waiting for my response, he continued, 'What do you want to do now?'

Given the frame of mind I had been in earlier that morning, I was initially tempted to say, 'Forget it!' Instead, to my surprise, I found myself replying, 'Go for it, Ralph – but you'll have to deal with it for now – I don't feel strong enough to cope with such matters at the moment.'

This news, coming as it did so very quickly after the prophetic statement I had heard on the television, was, I felt, more than just a coincidence. It also left me a little breathless. As far as everyone had been aware, that building was sold. The group we thought had purchased it had even applied for and received planning permission for alterations. We had received no communication from the estate agents for the previous two months. Now everything was cranking up again, just moments after I had heard what Benny Hinn had to say. God's timing is impeccable. It was as though God was saying that He *did* see me and what was happening to me – but for my part, I had to trust Him for the future. A verse from Isaiah came into my mind: "'For my thoughts are not your thoughts, neither are your ways my ways," declares the LORD. "As the heavens are higher than the earth, so are my ways higher than your ways and my thoughts than your thoughts'" (Isaiah 55:8-9).

Even as I began to dress, I instinctively knew that I had turned some kind of corner, or had got over an important hurdle. God was true to His Word – no weapon formed against me could prosper. I was protected by His armour, He was fighting my battles for me and leading me onwards. They say that it is always darkest before the dawn, and I felt I was just emerging from a very dark period of time, when I had been stretched to the very limit. Yet in that stretching I felt I had started to give birth to something that I still did not fully comprehend. And just like any natural birth, it had involved feelings of intense pain, which would continue until the delivery was complete. Now I felt sure that at the end of it all, new life would come forth – not just for me, but for many of whom I had no knowledge as yet. God had a plan and a purpose, and once more I knew that I was part of it. I had a future and a hope – in Him. Suddenly my tomorrows looked a whole lot brighter.

TWO

Humble beginnings

Although Bob and I had become financially prosperous by the time our marriage broke up, owning several properties in Britain and abroad, the early years of my life had been spent in far more modest surroundings. I was born in a small nursing home in Hornchurch, Essex, in the southeast corner of England, to working-class parents who at the time were living in rented accommodation. My dad, Alf Talbot, worked as a ticket clerk for British Railways, and my mother Emily worked as a home help to the elderly.

My parents' friendship began on board ship in 1930. My mother was on her way to Canada to work as cook in a large house in Quebec, having left her family behind in the north of England. Her father had died years before, when she was just three weeks old. I am told that he had a strong faith, was a member of a Salvation Army band, and could often be seen on the street corners of Tyneside playing his trumpet to the glory of God.

Mum was rather surprised to see Alf Talbot on board, having met him once before at a party. He was travelling back to Canada after living in England for some time, to rejoin his mother, sister and her family, who had moved there earlier. His father by this time had passed away.

Romance blossomed as Alf and Emily spent time relaxing together on the lengthy voyage, and by the time their long journey had ended they had established a close relationship and decided to keep in touch by letter. Although that could have been just a vague promise, they did in fact correspond with each other, and I now have in my possession several letters that Mum wrote to Dad, which came to light again only when he died.

Mum's letters, which cover a period of about one month immediately after she first arrived in Quebec, tell of the intense loneliness of starting a new job in a strange country, her worries about whether she would be able to carry out all her many duties adequately, and then, as she got into the job, the different chores she had to carry out each day. In one letter she says that she had just finished for the day at 10.30 p.m., having started at 6.30 a.m!

She writes about the awfully hot temperatures in the kitchen, which caused her clothes to be wringing wet with perspiration, and of her concern about the butler, who she felt might be taking a liking to her, and about her employer, who was intensely annoyed when she came back to the house one evening later than pleased him. The final letters tell how she plans to leave 'the big house' and find fresh employment elsewhere, because the servant quarters were found to be infested with bed bugs – the final straw as far as she was concerned.

The recurring theme of her letters, however, is her deep affection for Alf, and she says how much she misses him, describing how, if he were able to get her a job near him, she would come 'just like a bunny after lettuce'.

My father initially took work in Windsor, Ontario, and lodged with a relative by the name of Mrs Dunlop. But Mum and Dad both eventually ended up living near the rest of his family in Port Arthur, Ontario, which is now called Thunder Bay. They were married there on Christmas Day 1930. Historical records show that the snow was 10 feet deep that day.

Within three years of falling in love and marrying, they were back in England. Mum was expecting their first child, a boy, whom they called James Edward. It was the Depression in Canada that had brought them back to England, but without realizing it they had gone from one difficult monetary situation to another, as there was also a slump in the British economy when they arrived. Having very little money and no immediate job prospects, they lodged for a while with some of Dad's relatives in

East London, until something a little more permanent could be sorted out.

Family life

My brother is nearly 11 years older than I am, and was in full-time employment before I even started primary school. My first recollections of him involve him going off on his bike with his friends, and bringing me sweets when he came home from work. He would always buy fireworks on Bonfire Night, something that Dad considered a waste of money but which pleased me, especially as it was my birthday the following day.

It has to be said that my parents were more than a little surprised when they discovered that I was on the way. There were several reasons for this. First of all, my mother had reached the age of 43, when most women of her generation would be considered too old to be able to conceive a child. The other reason was that, due to the war, my father was away more than he was home, making the unlikely event of them becoming parents for a second time even more far-fetched.

Mum first voiced her suspicions to Dad, before making an appointment to see her local GP. Even he did not believe her initially, as her medical records stated that she was unable to bear any more children. In spite of everyone's doubts, she was proved right, and when I was born on Saturday 6 November 1943 I was referred to as 'the miracle baby' by the staff at the nursing home – something that made me feel very special when I heard the story retold as I grew up.

My Dad was an accountant, and was great at mental arithmetic. He was able to add up rows and rows of figures in his head in record time without ever making a mistake. Yet the only qualifications he had came from his work for Canadian Railways, qualifications that were not recognized in Britain at that time. This obstacle stopped him from getting a job which would have paid a good wage.

Maybe that was one of the reasons why he was drawn towards gambling. Each year he went on holiday for one week to Monte Carlo, on his own, to try his luck at the gaming tables. More often than not he lost, which made him rather miserable when he came back. You could tell instantly by the look on his face. If he had possessed more money, I am sure he would have been a big-time gambler.

The difficult situations he had experienced made him honest, methodical, tidy, careful with his money, but also a bit on the mean side. Mum never knew exactly how much he earned each week, as he was very secretive about the amount he was paid. The 1930s were terrible times to live through, and undoubtedly he had seen much hardship. This caused him to keep as much of what he earned as he could, in case other rainy days came along.

He ended up giving Mum the very least amount of housekeeping money he could get away with. Yet, in spite of his tendency to hold on to what he had, he never seemed to have any spare money, and was always waiting for the next pay day to arrive. I guess today's generation find it difficult to understand what it was like to live through a major economic depression, followed by a war, when everything was rationed and in short supply.

That must have coloured Dad's thinking on a lot of things, including money. Even I can still remember ration books, and the need to take them to a sweet shop before the goodies could be handed over, as rationing in Britain did not cease totally until 1954. So, although Dad found it difficult to be generous, there were very real circumstances which affected his thoughts and actions.

Mum, however, was just the opposite in that respect. She was a cook by profession, and had a real heart for people. When she was working as a home help, she would often work way beyond her hours just because she had a genuine love for the old people in her care. Sometimes she would even stay overnight with them when they were sick, which used to annoy Dad as she was not paid any extra money for doing it. She worked very hard for very little financial gain.

In spite of this, unlike Dad, she always seemed to have money in her purse, and enough to give to those who were in need. Looking back, I believe this made a big impression on me, as I began to understand at an early age the biblical principle spelled out in Luke 6:38: 'Give, and it will be given to you. A good measure, pressed down, shaken together and running over, will be poured into your lap. For with the measure you use, it will be measured to you' (NIV). She probably would not have been able to quote chapter and verse, even though she had been brought up in the Church of England, but she did better than that – she lived it out on a daily basis.

When I met Bob years later, I found that the same principle had been worked into his life too. There was more than one occasion after we first started going out together when he would feel compelled to empty the entire contents of his wallet anonymously through the letterbox of someone he knew was in great need. On several occasions, having given away every penny he had on him, he managed to get a lift for me from one of our friends, only to find that there was no room in the car for himself. He would then have to walk several miles home, on his own, sometimes in the pouring rain, but happy in the knowledge that he had done what he felt the Lord was telling him to do. Maybe it was because Bob was free to give away the little he had when prompted by God that God was free to trust Bob and me with so much in later years.

Mum got the job of school cook at the primary school I attended, and promptly changed all the rules regarding the use of powdered milk and eggs, which the school had used up to that point, insisting instead on fresh, wholesome ingredients. This did not make her popular to begin with, but soon the value of what she advocated was recognized, and the rules she laid down stayed long after she left that job.

When school was over, her cooking skills were required just as much, if not more, at home. She used to bake cakes by the dozen, only to have them eaten by my brother and his friends, who would nip through the back door and devour them as fast as she made them. Mum just saw that as approval of her talents and promptly set about making another batch.

My parents did not have any strong Christian beliefs when I was a child, but Mum had attended the local Anglican church near Gateshead as a girl, and I was sent off to the nearest Sunday School from a very early age. It happened to be run by the Plymouth Brethren, a Protestant group who placed great emphasis on Bible reading and prayer, and leading a quiet and sober life. I knew little or nothing of their beliefs at the time, but loved going along, mainly because it was a chance to meet with my friends.

When I was almost seven we moved from the rented bungalow which had been home until that point, to a council house in Elm Park, a suburb of Hornchurch, on the other side of town. As council houses went, it was quite spacious and even had a downstairs toilet, which was almost unheard of in those days. Apart from the kitchen, we had two rooms downstairs – the living room, where most of our time was spent, and the 'front room', which was kept for special occasions or visitors. Both rooms had a fireplace and I can remember my parents and I staring at the flames dancing in the fireplace until the room got quite dark, when we were forced to turn on the electric light – having saved a little on electricity in the meantime, thus gaining Dad's approval.

I liked school and, although I was never destined to set the world on fire academically, I suppose it would be fair to say that I was termed 'average' in most subjects. Like all children, I had favourite subjects – and others that I wished had never been invented! The teachers at my primary school, Benhurst in Elm Park, did their very best to get me enthused about passing the 11-plus so that I could go to grammar school. Most of my friends, however, had decided they did not wish to sit the exam, so I knew that if I did pass I would have to leave them all behind. Consequently, I am afraid that I did not make an awful lot of effort to prepare for the exam, and failed miserably.

I ended up attending Suttons Secondary Modern School in Hornchurch. I enjoyed our religious instruction classes, domestic science and music, and shone at English, spelling and mental arithmetic – but maths, geography and history left me cold. Officially I finished my education at 15, but in fact I stayed on to complete a commercial course, studying shorthand and typing, before going to work for May & Baker, a pharmaceutical company based in Dagenham.

I suppose that it is second nature for children coming in from school these days to switch on the television and watch their favourite programmes for a while, but I never did that as we did not have a television. This was more to do with Dad's beliefs than our economic situation. He was a member of the Noise Abatement Society and he considered television too time consuming and noisy, or at least that is what he told us. We did, however, have the very latest model of radio, which cost as much as a television but was presumably easier to control as far as sound was concerned – except when his beloved football team were playing, and then the volume would be turned up! My dad and brother, both avid supporters of West Ham, would often go to Upton Park to watch their team play their home matches.

Sunday was a time when we would often eat together as a family. By the time I was 13, my brother had married, and he and his wife would sometimes join us for Sunday lunch. On weekdays, however, I had often eaten before Dad came home from work, as he used to work shifts.

Even though I eventually married a man who would make a fortune from the motor industry, as a child I walked to school every day – but so did everyone else, with the possible exception of those children living a greater distance away, who used to hop on a bus. Although I had few luxuries as a child, one annual treat was our two-week holiday, compliments of British Railways. As part of his job package, Dad was given 'privilege tickets' for travelling around Britain, plus one overseas ticket which was absolutely free. When I was 13 I went with my parents to Austria by train. I was the envy of my class when I returned, as I told them how we had slept on the train during the night hours. Today, with so much cheap and easy travel available, it is strange to recall that not many ordinary families travelled abroad in the 1950s.

Encounter with God

Moving from one part of town to the other meant that it was too far to go to my old Sunday School, although I still attended if something special had been arranged or if I happened to be visiting friends in the area. I had really enjoyed going to the church, so at one point, when they had a series of meetings for children stretching over a week, I went every evening, even though it was a bus ride away and I had to pay the bus fare out of my meagre pocket money. Looking back, I realize that these were meetings geared for children just like me, who did not come from Christian families and who needed to know that God loved them and wanted them to invite Jesus into their hearts. The organizers preached a gospel message each evening, but did not make it clear how anyone interested in taking action on their message should respond. I remember coming home at the end of the week and crying in my bedroom because I knew I needed God in my life, but I still did not know what to do next! I dug out an old Bible belonging to my dad and tried to read a little of it every night, but I soon gave up and forgot all about it.

God had not forgotten me, however, and a few months later, as I was coming out of school with a friend of mine called Valerie, a middle-aged lady started to chat to us. She invited us to come along to a new Sunday School that was going to start the following week at an assembly hall nearby which was often used for functions such as wedding receptions. There was something about the lady that we both trusted, and we were interested enough to take up her invitation when the day rolled round.

Valerie and I went along together that first Sunday afternoon, and soon we were going on a regular basis. The Sunday School superintendent was a young man called Terry O'Neill. At this point Terry was still living at home with his parents and was courting a young lady called Margaret. After a few weeks he began inviting a few of us to tea every Sunday at his parents' house before taking us along to the evening service at the main church in Dagenham. This meant a trip on a tube train for two stations, which all seemed very exciting at the time. At the end of the service we made the return journey home, escorted by Terry and Margaret.

Terry's mum and dad made us feel very welcome and special, and gave us the most delicious tea. Soon a dozen or more young people were making the trip each week. Every so often we were taken to even bigger meetings that the church supported, held at the Albert Hall and preceded by a big, open-air rally in Trafalgar Square. In spite of the fact that Terry's mum had a lovely home which she kept spotlessly clean, she did not seem to worry at all about a horde of youngsters invading it every Sunday. In fact, she welcomed us all with open arms. Without the love and care of Terry, his mum and dad and Margaret, I doubt whether I would be a Christian today. Nothing was too much trouble for them and they always had time for us. I now realize that people can be generous in every area of their lives – it need not just be confined to money. Time, thoughts and attitudes can all have a generosity tag attached to them and, as the Bible says, 'God loves a cheerful giver' (2 Corinthians 9:7).

Finally I had found a church that not only preached the gospel but knew how to explain it to the searching heart of a child. I invited Jesus to take control of my life on Sunday 4 April 1954. Several of my friends, including

Valerie, took the same step that evening. Even though I was only 10 years old, my conversion was real, and I started to experience many changes in my life. I began to get Bible story books from the library, and the temptation to pinch loose biscuits from the local Woolworth's store was no longer there. God's Spirit started to take hold of my life, and I knew without doubt what it was to experience the peace of God, even at that young age.

My one desire was to get my family to experience what I had found to be true. It took me about two years to get my mother to come to a service at my church, but when she did she also asked Jesus into her life, and in turn introduced quite a few others to the Christian faith. True to form, Dad did not come even though he was often invited, but he never tried to stop Mum and me going along. I think he felt comforted that we were attending church on a regular basis, perhaps thinking that if we did, then it somehow let him off the hook.

Although I had been christened as an infant, when I was 14 I took the decision to be totally immersed in water. This is known as 'believer's baptism', which gives witness to the fact that someone has accepted Jesus into their heart, and intends to continue following His ways and doing His will.

The problem was that the pastor of the church in Dagenham, Alfred Webb, used to get me mixed up with another girl, whose name was Pauline. Sure enough, on the night of the baptism, as he lowered my entire body under the water he referred to me as Pauline. Feeling that it was important he should get my name right on this very special occasion, I came spluttering up from under the water and managed to gasp, 'I'm Pat – not Pauline!' Looking slightly embarrassed, he promptly went through the whole procedure again, this time using my correct name. Not many can say that they have been baptized twice on the same night!

The church had high moral standards for all its members. Smoking and drinking were out, and so were make-up, dances and visits to the cinema. That sounds very restrictive, especially against today's liberal background, but I have to say that I never felt particularly deprived or constrained. I had a great bunch of friends and the church rules, which were implied rather than strictly enforced, probably kept me and my friends protected from the worst excesses of the 'Swinging Sixties', when standards in the cinema and theatre dropped alarmingly and drugs started to be introduced into the country. Nowadays I feel free to enjoy an evening at the cinema or theatre, but I rarely do, still getting most enjoyment from fellowship with other Christians.

Although my early teenage years were carefree, less happy days were to follow. Dad became ill with cancer in 1962 – although in those days cancer was not spoken about by the doctors until they were forced to do so, and we therefore did not know for a long time that the 'duodenal ulcer' that he had was actually cancer of the colon. He had obviously guessed, however, and began to wonder about what would happen to him when he died. He asked to see both my pastor and my mother's pastor and they went together to see him in hospital. They told Dad how to find his peace with God and how to know for sure where he would go should he die, and Dad gave his life to the Lord there and then. Mum and I saw an instant change in him.

He said he was going to start reading a chapter of the Bible each day, beginning with the Gospel of Matthew. Five days later, he died. When we came to collect his things from the hospital, Mum noticed that the bookmark in the Bible he had been given was at the fifth chapter of Matthew. Both she and I knew that in the nick of time Dad had found Jesus to be Saviour and Lord, and that took away some of the pain of losing him. I was still only 18 years old.

How I met Bob

By this time a church had been formed in the town where I lived as a 'branch' from the main Dagenham church. Terry O'Neill, now married to Margaret, became the pastor. This meant that I no longer had to trek over to Dagenham for every meeting. The church seemed to consist predominantly of young people at this time, although later some older people started to join too. The young people were in fact all girls, 12 of us to be exact.

We all loved going to the Fellowship, but became increasingly aware of the distinct lack of males within our church. I think our pastor was aware too that, if the situation did not change, we would gradually drift off to other fellowships, or maybe no fellowship at all if we found boyfriends who were not connected with a church. He therefore encouraged us to pray for young men to start coming on a Sunday. Believing with all our hearts that God hears us when we pray (a thing that I have proved time and time again in my Christian life), we began to ask the Lord for men – young men – to join our fellowship.

Guess who was first on the scene? An extremely shy Bob Edmiston, who blushed bright red when he had to shake hands with us all, as we lined up to say hello. It was apparently his dad's idea that he came along: although he did not attend a church regularly, he had an enquiring mind about all kinds of things, including religion, and he brought Bob along to check us out. Ours was the church he 'just happened' to choose only a short while after we had started praying for young men to invade us! I still find it amazing that Bob did not simply turn on his heels and run within the first five minutes, as he was confronted with a dozen giggly teenage girls, obviously eyeing him up. But he stayed and, although I did not know it then, I had met the man who would be my husband for 30 years and the father of my three children.

Soon other young men joined Bob, and at first we all tended to go around together as one big group. I was over two and a half years older than Bob and had no idea at all that he was interested in me. He would ask my friend Lyn if she could tell him what bus or train I would be catching the next day, and then suddenly I would find him by my side, chatting away about anything or nothing. I had got so used to seeing Bob chatting to Lyn, however, that I reckoned he must really like her, not guessing for quite some time that he was actually trying to find out from her what my next moves were! Gradually the one big group split into several smaller ones, and in the end Lyn, Bob, a chap called David Smith and I formed a foursome.

Eventually this shy but very likeable young man made his feelings for me known, and we started going out together at the end of 1965. Bob got on well with my mum, who loved it when he teased her. I in turn got on reasonably well with his mum and dad, although I remember feeling rather nervous the first few times I met them. I think they did have some reservations about their young teenage son going out with a somewhat older woman – the age difference seemed quite a gap at that time of life.

We decided to get engaged on Bob's twentieth birthday. He was very mature for his age and had all kinds of ideas about what he was going to do with his life, some of which included making money, while others were to do with sharing his Christian faith. I was actually earning more than Bob at this stage, working in London for Clerical Medical and General Life Insurance as a shorthand typist. Bob was a bank clerk for the English Scottish and Australian Bank.

Bob had a thing about cars. Any cars. They did not have to be a certain model or make. Old cars, beaten-up cars, end-of-the-road cars – he saw them all as potential for earning a few extra pounds. He would spend hours with a friend of his fixing the engine or doing up the bodywork, and then would sell the cars for a few pounds more than he had paid for them. More often than not he would treat us to a Chinese meal with the profits – or give the money away to someone who needed it more. The first car that Bob ever owned was a far cry from the kind of vehicle he drives today. He bought it in 1966, the year that he passed his driving test. It was a 1952 Ford Popular – the 'sit up and beg' type – which cost the princely sum of £18 and lasted all of two weeks. Mind you, in spite of its age, it did have automatic windows: every time he went over a bump, they automatically fell down.

Bob was very serious about his walk with God, just as I was serious about mine. There were also other things that we had in common. I played the piano at church – in a very amateur way at first until I took piano lessons. Bob played bass guitar with a group of lads about the same age as him, all of whom by this time had joined our church. They were once invited to play with a group in Trafalgar Square at an open-air rally, and they stood by the statues of the lions and sang for the Lord. It was a special and memorable occasion.

Now we were engaged. Bob and I spent a lovely evening at a local Indian restaurant with both our families, celebrating our engagement. That night just before I switched off the light, I took one final glance at the beautiful solitaire engagement ring Bob had given me, and sensed that life was going to be far from dull now that I had agreed to marry Bob. As I snuggled down between the sheets, however, I could not have guessed just how right my instincts would prove to be.

THREE

Cars, kids and Chinese meals

Suddenly, there seemed so much to do. Bob and I were due to marry on Saturday 23 September 1967, 12 months after our engagement. The church had to be booked, guests invited, bridesmaids chosen, Bob had to recruit a best man, and our honeymoon arrangements also needed to be made.

We decided to hold our wedding service at the church my mother was attending, the Elim Pentecostal Church in Romford, Essex. Our Fellowship met in a hired hall, and the main church in Dagenham was in the middle of a massive building programme, hence our decision to use another church. The building itself was nothing special – it held about 120 people at a pinch, was brick built and of simple design inside and out. But with some imaginative flower arrangements – which, come the day, I failed to notice – I knew it would be very friendly and inviting.

I decided that I would like to have three bridesmaids, one of them being Bob's sister Viv, who was a similar age to me and was living and working in Germany at the time, plus two young girls who were pupils in my Sunday School class – Ellen and Christine, who were about 15 and had been in my class since the age of six. I would have liked very much to have had my friend Lyn as a bridesmaid, but she was already committed to attending her parents' silver wedding celebrations on that day.

Money was tight, to say the least. Dad had died five years before, and Mum had been forced to stop working because of ill health, which made me the only breadwinner in the house. It was my responsibility to pay all the household bills, as my brother had his own family to provide for by that time. Although Mum insisted on paying for the invitations, Bob and I had to foot the bill for the rest of the wedding, and that was very much dependent on what we could comfortably afford.

In spite of the financial restrictions that faced us, we wanted as many of our friends and family to be there as possible, and the final number of guests who shared in our special day was around 80. Apart from Viv and her German boyfriend Adolf, nobody had really travelled very far, as many of our relatives lived within the Greater

London area. We both had family members living overseas who were not able to come, however, and they very kindly sent telegrams, which were duly read out before the speeches.

I could not afford to have a wedding dress specially designed and made for me, as many brides do today, but I managed to find an off-the-peg number that I really liked. It was quite simple in design, with a straight skirt and a guipure lace bodice. A long train gave it that final touch. But it was £40 – a lot more than I should really have been spending on a dress. One could do a lot with £40 in those days! After much debate with myself, I bought it anyway, but was reluctant to tell Bob just how much I had paid for it for some time afterwards. I then chose some beautiful white shoes which had very high stiletto heels, in an effort to bring myself a little more up to Bob's height. He is almost a foot taller than me.

My mother was given the keys to the church before the wedding day, as her pastor was not taking any part in our service. We were being married by our own pastor, Mike Godward, who had taken over when Terry O'Neill moved on to take charge of another church. We naturally wanted everything to be just right, with any possible hitches sorted out ahead of the big day. Nonetheless, on the morning of the wedding my little nephew Paul, who was only three, arrived at the house with his parents and somehow got hold of the church keys – and then promptly managed to lose them. That was the last thing we needed, and it did not do much for the nerves! After a manic game of hide and seek the keys remained lost, and there was nothing for it but to head off to the church, wondering whether we would even be able to get into the building. As the wedding car turned into the street where the church was, I realized with great relief that all was well. The church organist had been given a duplicate set of keys, and had saved the day.

Apart from that nerve-jangling start, it was a very happy day and all the other arrangements went very much according to plan. Bob had his brother Mike as his best man, and my brother Ted proudly gave me away. He did a fine job, but I remember feeling a tinge of sadness as I left the house. I could not help thinking how Dad would have loved to have been there to see his only daughter walk down the aisle. It is, after all, an occasion that most fathers very much look forward to.

After the marriage ceremony and the normal lengthy photograph session, we set off for the reception, which was held in a hired hall a few miles away in Rainham. We had arranged for a sit-down meal to be served to our guests, which consisted of cold meat and salad and a desert – at a cost of 7/6d a head, about 35p in today's money. As I said earlier, money seemed to go very much further in those days.

We left for our honeymoon at around 9 o'clock in the evening, when the wedding reception was nearly over and we had managed brief chats with all our friends and relatives. We had booked a two-week holiday in Cornwall, staying in a mobile home. Being September, it was dark by the time we set off. Rather than make the whole long journey to Cornwall at that late hour in our not-too-reliable 1960 Ford Consul, we decided to break our journey at some point, and then continue the next morning.

By the time we got to Reading in Berkshire, we both felt we had done enough mileage for one evening and agreed to look round for somewhere to spend the night. We knocked on the door of the first house that looked reasonable and displayed a bed and breakfast sign. The door was opened by a middle-aged, one-eyed woman who confirmed that she had a room to let, then led us up the stairs to a rather cold and damp bedroom. It was not the most auspicious start to our married life, but we both reasoned, once she had left us alone, that it was only for one night.

The next morning, after a full English breakfast, we paid our bill and headed off to where we had parked our car, only to see, in the full light of day, the wonderful handiwork wrought by our friends and family at the wedding reception the night before. Balloons, string, confetti, streamers and graffiti were all over the car. Not having realized the full extent of what they had done, we had blithely parked on the main road outside the guesthouse. We beat a hasty retreat, in a cloud of embarrassment and amusement, while the landlady watched us from behind the lace curtains with her one eye.

It was good just to spend time together and to enjoy the Cornish countryside after the rush and bustle leading up to the wedding. Our lives were already full, with our work and church commitments, and we both appreciated time away from family and friends to relax together and to begin to get to know each other better, at the beginning of our married life.

Home concerns

We travelled back from Cornwall the day before Bob's twenty-first birthday. No big celebration was planned as he had seen most of his friends at the wedding, and we could not really afford another big get-together so soon afterwards. The mail that was waiting for us proved the point. Mixed up among the late cards of congratulations which had arrived while we were away was a notification from the bank that several of the cheques we had written to pay for items associated with the wedding had bounced. We quickly had to do some careful thinking and budgeting to get everything sorted out. In truth, we did not have a bean between us, and it was a continual balancing act to keep our bank accounts from going too far into the red.

Not all the news that we received on our return was bad. We were thrilled to hear that Viv and Adolf had announced their engagement on the day after our wedding, and were planning their own big day nine months later.

In spite of the fact that we were struggling financially, we both believed that it was right to give a tenth of everything we earned back to God. It was our strong conviction that, according to biblical principles, if we honoured God by giving back to Him a tenth of what we had, He would make sure that we were never in want. The belief is rooted in the early part of the Old Testament, when Abraham, returning from a battle, meets a mysterious priest called Melchizedek and gives a tenth of what he has won in the battle to him. Because of that act, God was able to bless and prosper Abraham all through his life. Many Bible scholars believe that Melchizedek represents Jesus and that, just as Abraham gave a tenth to Melchizedek, it is right to give a tenth of what we have earned back to God. We also believed that this was right. Although it was a financial struggle at the time, God did provide for us, and He met our needs in a wonderful way as the months and years went by.

We had nowhere to live at this point, although we had viewed a semi-detached house in Rainham just a couple of months before. We liked the house very much and felt it would be suitable for our first home, and we put in what we felt was a reasonable bid. This was duly accepted and everything seemed to be going through normally, but then we were told a few days before our wedding that someone else had put in a higher bid. We had been gazumped. When we returned from honeymoon, therefore, we quickly had to find somewhere to live. After staying with my mother for about a week, we heard of a reasonably priced one-bedroomed flat to rent in Ilford, several miles away from where our parents lived. It was not the place of our dreams – in fact, there was not much that was nice about it – yet we reckoned that it was probably the best we could afford at that point, and told the landlord that we would move in immediately.

It was part of a big house that had been divided into flats, and ours was the first room down the corridor. It was far from ideal. If we wanted to eat in privacy, we had to walk across a courtyard from the kitchen to the dining room, which meant it was almost impossible to get a hot meal in cold weather. But at least it was a roof over our heads. We did not know it at the time, of course, but the address of this property offered a clue to the part of the country where we would spend the majority of our married life: the flat was in Coventry Road, and Coventry was where we would ultimately move to, and where we would spend many happy years.

Then, to our total surprise and delight, after two months in that dingy little flat, the property next door to the house we had originally wanted came on the market. Not only was it more suited to our requirements, it was also slightly cheaper than the first house! So we were at last able to move into our very first home. It was such an exciting time for us.

Needless to say, we had to go for a 100 per cent mortgage as there were no funds available to use as a deposit. In fact, I think we had a sum total of £11 in the bank between us at that time. Then we had to face the question of how we were going to furnish the property now that we had acquired it. We both disliked the idea of credit or hire purchase, which would have increased our weekly outgoings considerably. We need not have worried, however. God once again wonderfully undertook for us and provided everything we needed at a price we could afford.

Some friends of ours were moving away, and needed to get rid of some of their furniture and other household goods. They offered us a three-piece suite, a bed, a twin-tub washing machine, an iron, a cooker and a sideboard as well as a dining room table and chairs. They also threw in a carpet for our little living room which, although not fitted, at least covered the centre of the floor, leaving a border of polished floorboards. We managed to furnish our entire house for the princely sum of £40! I could not help thinking, as the furniture was being put into place, that I had spent that same amount on just one dress. I reasoned, however, that it was a very special dress, and it was the only wedding dress I ever intended to buy.

Our new home had no garage, so Bob decided to build one as our car was rather old, did not start very easily and therefore needed to be kept under cover. He set about it with great enthusiasm, but not much else! Whenever he had a spare hour or two, which was not very often, he would try to add a few more layers of bricks to the construction and eventually, after several months, he proudly declared it finished. As we stood back to admire his work, we both wondered how long it would stay up, as the line of the bricks seemed to have a distinctly wavy aspect. Nonetheless, in fairness to Bob I should say that the garage is, as far as I know, still standing today. I believe, however, that Bob has never laid another brick since!

Treats were few and far between at the start of our married life. Occasionally we would buy a Chinese takeaway, a comparative rarity in those days. Money was indeed tight and Bob had a novel way of picking up some extra money to pay for our tasty treats. Once again, it was all connected to his fascination with cars.

Our pastor, Mike Godward, had an uncle who owned a garage. He used to have old cars come into his possession from time to time and Mike would get hold of the old bangers, do them up, and then sell them on for a small profit. Mike invited Bob to get involved, on the under- standing that they could share the work and split the prof- its. From then on, many spare hours were spent working away on the vehicles, which sometimes were hardly worth all the time and energy the two men lavished on them. Yet they would always try to get them looking as good as they could, and would simply hope that their latest labour of love would start when a customer came to view it. If they had any doubts, they would get the engine turning over and then keep it running until the customer arrived.

Bob was involved in so many activities – including night school, youth work and his own day job – that he could sometimes be found shoving old cars along the street at 3 a.m. My skills were sometimes called upon – as an extra pair of hands to push a car along in an attempt to get it started. Even when I was seven months pregnant, I sat in the driving seat of a big old Jaguar, trying to steer it straight while the men pushed it. I had only just passed my driving test, but the good people of Dagenham need not have worried, as I was only travelling at a few miles per hour. It was a very heavy vehicle, being shoved with much effort along a very busy road! Inevitably, all our ill- gotten gains – or should I say the men's hard labour? – was spent on a Chinese takeaway treat, after which they would start looking around for the next car to work on.

Cooking for the two of us was not the ordeal for me that some new wives experience. Due to the kind of work that she did, Mum was sometimes not around to start an evening meal when I lived at home, so I got used to preparing the vegetables and cooking the potatoes, having picked up a few of her cooking skills. By the time I married, I knew how to put a reasonably tasty meal together. It was all pretty basic stuff, though – my dad had been a meat and two veg man. Bob enjoyed more exotic fare, including a good curry and other rice-based dishes, as well as Chinese food. After a while, therefore, I began to experiment. On one or two occasions at the beginning, I managed to burn the rice and promptly disposed of it before anyone saw it, but I learned quickly, and enjoyed trying out new foods. Bob's mum was also great at giving me hints on how to cook some of the more exotic dishes. Her tips and expert advice saw me through many culinary dilemmas.

Both Bob and I became fully involved in the life of our little church. I was the church pianist and a Sunday School teacher, while Bob was involved in the youth work and played the guitar in a group. The group were good, and managed to get themselves fairly well known locally. They were sometimes requested to play at various church events, some of which were very large gatherings. Bob loved the guitar and learned to play really well. As money started to become less of a problem for us, he was able to buy several guitars, some of them quite rare and expensive.

As the months went past, we fell into a busy routine of going to work, rushing to a mid-week meeting or the youth group, buying and selling those old cars and generally trying to keep the financial wolf from the door. It would not always be like that, we felt. Bob was ambitious, and wanted to get on in his career as much as he could.

Children – an inheritance from the Lord

About 14 months after we were married, we discovered that I was expecting our first child. We were both delighted, and started to make all the preparations necessary for the new arrival. It was a fairly straightforward pregnancy, and I was eventually admitted to Rush Green Hospital in Romford for the birth. In spite of my small frame, I was duly delivered of a nine-and-a-half-pound baby boy – who was promptly nicknamed 'The Whopper' by the nursing staff. For some reason, women did not seem to have big babies very often in those days. We decided to call him Andrew. We both wanted a biblical name, and Andrew was the first one that we both liked.

Andrew was born on Sunday 13 July 1969, which was the very day the doctor had said that he was due. It was during the time that preparations for the Apollo 11 space mission dominated the news. The United States launched Apollo 11 towards the moon on 16 July. On 20 July, astronauts Neil A. Armstrong and Edwin E. Aldrin Jr walked on the moon's surface. As Armstrong took his first step, he radioed a message to the world: 'That's one small step for a man, one giant leap forward for mankind.' I watched the broadcasts on the hospital television, with our new son cradled in my arms, and wondered what the future had in store for him, and for the rest of mankind.

The birth took place at around 9 p.m., with Bob in attendance. Neither of us cared what gender our first child was, so long as it was healthy, but I was secretly pleased that I had supplied Bob with a son. Later that night, or in the early hours of the following morning, I woke up with a jump. For a moment I did not know where I was, then I remembered. A tingle of excitement went through my body as I reminded myself that I was now a mother. I can still remember the tremendous thrill of that moment to this day.

The day that Armstrong uttered his famous words about one giant leap for mankind was the day that I was discharged from hospital. I was now a mother of a beautiful son – a considerable personal step, I felt! Hospital attitudes were very different towards pregnancy and the needs of mothers after a birth at that time, and I was hospitalized for a whole week before I was allowed to begin the task of looking after our son in our own home.

My mother came round to help me for a day or two, and Bob took a few days off work, but after that I was on my own. There had been no big decision to make about whether I should give up work or not. Generally speaking, if it was at all possible, women were expected to concentrate on looking after their babies themselves in those days.

For the first little while after Andrew came home from hospital, I never seemed to have a moment to get any housework done. He was the kind of baby you could set your clock by as far as feeding was concerned. They said at the hospital that he would probably need feeding every three hours, and sure enough, he would wake for his feed, not a minute before or after. It was quite uncanny, especially as he was also born on the very day he was due. (I have to say that this punctuality trait is not one that lasted into later life.) Despite this conveniently regular feeding pattern, however, there never seemed to be time for anything else. By the time I had dealt with the terry-towelling nappies, hung them and any other washing out to dry, filled the sterilizing unit with various implements and grabbed a hurried cup of coffee, Andrew was awake again and the whole process began once more. For a while we seemed to live in total disorder, until I was able to get back into some kind of routine. Initially I would feel a little embarrassed when someone would come to visit unexpectedly and the house was not up to my normal tidy standard, but my new responsibility was worth all the temporary disorder. It was a lovely period of my life.

I was unexpectedly back in hospital with Andrew later on that year – Christmas Day to be exact – but thankfully not as a patient. Due to constant pain from arthritis, Mum had undergone a hip replacement operation and we went to see her on Christmas Day to cheer her up, taking her little grandson with us as a special surprise.

Life moved on, as Bob pursued his career and I looked after our home. Then, on Sunday 14 February 1971, we were blessed with the arrival of our second child – a daughter whom we named Debbie. She was also born at a memorable point in history: apart from it being Valentine's Day, it was also the time of the changeover from the old pounds, shillings and pence to decimal currency. Debbie was even bigger than Andrew, weighing in at around 10 pounds and already looking a month old when she was born. She brought great delight to us both, and now that we had a boy and a girl we felt that our family was complete. We had at that time no intention of having any more children.

Fortunately for us, God had a different plan. Much to our surprise and delight, four years later another daughter, Angela, arrived on the scene, also weighing in at 10 pounds. She was born very early on a Monday morning, on 20 January 1975. By this time we were living in the Midlands. It was great having the children around, and we used to have lots of fun together. All three were taken to church from just a few days old and joined the Sunday School as soon as they were able to.

Christmas was always a very special time in our home. I had always loved that part of the year and really did everything possible to make it special for all of us, with a tree in the living room and plenty of good things to eat. Bob's parents always joined us on Christmas Day and his dad enjoyed dressing up as Santa Claus and then handing out presents to us all. For years, the children never seemed to realize that Granddad was never around when Father Christmas appeared – or maybe they were just reluctant to spoil a family tradition by asking too many questions!

The move north

After we moved to the Midlands, our financial position started to improve as Bob's career began to take off. He soon had several promotions under his belt. When we first moved in August 1971, we lived in a house in Rugby, Warwickshire, and initially started to go to a little Pentecostal church in the same town. We did not really feel that this was where we should settle long term, however, and we began to look for another more suitable fellowship. We eventually decided to join a church in Keresley, about 15 miles away in the northern part of Coventry, where the services were similar to those we had attended in the past. There were many young people there and we felt it would be much more suitable for a growing family. Nevertheless, it did mean that we had to travel from Rugby to Coventry several times a week, as we eventually became closely involved in the life of the church.

After a few months of this, it seemed sensible to try to find a house a little nearer our place of worship, and we eventually found one that we both liked in a very pleasant part of Coventry. The only problem was that the people who were living in the property did not actually want to move for another year. We agreed with them the price we would pay when the move eventually took place, and then we continued to travel from Rugby to the church in Coventry for the next 12 months.

We did not put our own house on the market until several months later, however, and within that time house prices soared. We were therefore able to get a much better price for our house in Rugby than we would have done some months earlier. In fact, the price of the house we were selling had more than doubled, while we were still only paying the price we had previously agreed for the house in Coventry. It was 1973, the year the property boom started in Britain. Another factor in our favour was that we had moved from the prosperous South to the less wealthy Midlands. Everything seemed to be on our side.

Bob's dad had always advised him to invest any money he might have in property because it was, in his words, 'a very safe investment'. We were now beginning to benefit from his wise words. It was good to be a little more financially secure, but it probably helped our stability that it did not happen overnight. So often we read of people who have 'come into money' suddenly, and the pressures it brings sometimes prove to be much more than they can handle. Of course we had absolutely no inkling at that time of how financial success would sweep us into a very different lifestyle, or of the fact that there would also be a very heavy price to pay.

FOUR

Bob – the man
I married

No man or woman is called to be an island. As we journey through life we mix with, influence and are influenced by others. Each of us takes part in weaving the tapestry of the lives around us. There are many such people who have helped to shape me into the woman I am today, but none has had such an influence as Bob, and, although he obviously features throughout my story, in this chapter I want to tell you about the man I fell in love with in my early twenties and was married to for over 30 years.

Robert Norman Edmiston was born in New Delhi, India, on 6 October 1946, to Vivian Randolph and

Norma Margaret Mary Edmiston. He was a middle child, having an older sister called Vivanae and a younger brother called Michael, who was born several years after Bob. His father had been a wartime fighter pilot and was based in India working as an airline pilot when Bob was born.

By the time Bob was three years old he was fluent in Hindustani. His time in India, however, did not last very long as the country received independence from Britain and the family reluctantly found it necessary to leave. After exploring several different avenues, they eventually decided to come to England, the country of their origin. They arrived during the colder months and apparently found the weather to be something of a challenge!

As their third child was due to be born later that year, their first task was to find somewhere for the family to live and set up home. They lived for some time with relatives, and then in rented accommodation in the London area, before they were able to move to their own newly purchased property in Essex, where they remained for several years.

In 1956, when Bob was only 10 years old, it was all change for him yet again as his father had secured a job as a bush pilot in Kenya, which meant that the family had to move to Nairobi. It was necessary for his father to go on ahead several months earlier, leaving his mother with the task of selling up the family home as well as making all the necessary travel arrangements and preparing three young children for a move across continents. Later his father took another job in Nairobi, this time as the manager of Embekasi Airport.

A mixed education

Bob unashamedly admits that he struggled as far as education was concerned, often finding himself bottom, or at best amongst the lowest few in his class. This, of course, could have been due to the numerous times he played truant from school. He seemed to find many more interesting things to do with his time than merely sitting in a stuffy classroom. We always found it very amusing, during our family times together, when Bob related the story of how he and another boy called George regularly used to be present at school when the register was marked in the morning, and then did a disappearing act for the rest of the day. They got up to all sorts of mischief, such as lassoing the Governor's horses at State House and riding them off into the bush.

Another way Bob would while away the hours when he should have been at school involved picking flowers from the roundabout in town and then selling them for cash to unsuspecting households as he went from house to house, in order to supplement his weekly pocket money. It must have been the entrepreneur in him manifesting itself even at that young age. He would sometimes even implicate his brother Mike, who, being four years younger than Bob, was very easy to lead astray. The only problem with little brothers is that they do not always know what keeping a secret really means!

However Bob had secretly spent his time during school hours, he always made absolutely sure he was standing on the school steps each night when his mum and dad, who were completely oblivious of his antics, arrived to pick him up. His out-of-school activities went on for at least six months, until finally a teacher rumbled him and phoned his stunned parents. I can assure you that Bob still vividly remembers the outcome of that chapter in his life very well indeed.

His lack of educational progression and his diminished presence at school took their toll, and Bob was later kept down a class with children a year younger – something that really hurt his pride. It paid off, however, as in that class he was at least in the top few and he soon made up for lost time.

Bob mostly attended Catholic schools both in England and in East Africa. His mother was a member of the Catholic Church, which in those days favoured a strict regime. Being a mischievous child, he was often disciplined by the priests for the things he did, which did not help with any positive thoughts he might have had towards God at the time. Bob returned to England with the rest of his family when he was 15, after which he continued his education in England until the age of 17.

It was about this time that we were praying at our church for young men to join. Bob and his father, who was a nominal adherent of the Church of England and was interested in finding out more about other branches of the Christian Church, started to come along. Bob often recalled that their first visit was a direct result of an invitation they had received through the letterbox, although he did not know who was responsible for delivering it. His dad was the first to respond to the invitation, and he then encouraged Bob to accompany him. We always felt this was all in God's plan and purpose, as there was no way Bob would have made the first move. He was attending a Catholic church at the time, and he certainly would not have come anywhere near the place had he known that the entire youth group was made up of girls!

The learning establishments that Bob had attended had mainly all been boys' schools, and he was therefore very shy of the opposite sex – especially when almost a dozen girls lined up to shake his hand as soon as he arrived on the scene. Nonetheless, he testifies that in this little Pentecostal church he found a place where people were happy, genuinely believed in God and knew the Lord personally. He also discovered that they had an image of God entirely different from the one with which he had grown up. This was to make a big impact on him.

The way Bob became a Christian was quite dramatic. The year was 1963 and he was 17 years old. After leaving an evening youth meeting, he walked down the dark alleyway attached to the church and saw clearly in his mind's eye Jesus on the cross. At that moment, he understood that Jesus had died for him personally. Bob felt a need to give his life to God, and things began to change for him from that moment onwards. He began to get to know Jesus as a real person, and he developed a personal relationship with Him. Swearing, which had been a habit of his, ceased immediately, and his outlook on life became quite different. He was now living for God and not just himself. Bob and I were just good friends at this stage, and we did not go out together as a couple until some two years after his conversion. During that time many other young people, including more boys, joined the Fellowship.

Career moves

Bob had always wanted to travel, but was even willing to give up that idea if that was what God wanted. Little did he know at this point just how much travelling he would eventually have to do as he started to become increasingly successful in his career.

After Bob left school he went to work as a bank clerk with the English Scottish and Australian Bank in the City of London, where he stayed for about a year. He then started a job with US Steel – but was sacked after a few weeks because they found he did not have the knowledge they thought he had when they took him on. Bob apparently came over very well at the interview and appeared to be the ideal person for the job, although he knew it was a little beyond the experience he had at the time. Yet Bob had a very quick brain and felt that with a little help he would be able to fulfil the tasks required. That was not the case, however. From the very first day he was expected to know how to do the work and was not given any help or assistance at all. After leaving there he was convinced that, given a bit of tuition, he would be able to do that particular job, and so he applied for a similar post elsewhere to prove to himself, if nothing else, that he was capable. That new job proved to be a vital link to his future success.

This change of job began his career in the motor trade. He worked first for Chrysler, then for the Ford Motor Company, then returned to Chrysler. It was after a conversation with a training officer at Ford that Bob was inspired to get ahead in his career. He had been offered a job in insurance, but was advised by the training officer, in whom he confided, to forget the idea as he felt that Bob was more suited to the motor industry. It was shortly before this and while he was still working for Ford that our marriage took place.

However good his natural ability was, Bob knew that he needed training qualifications, having come out of school with just seven O levels. He therefore decided to attend night school three nights a week. We had been married for a couple of years by this time, and he now had a wife and baby son to support. To say that these were tough times is an understatement. Bob worked extremely hard and, as his workload increased considerably with the additional studying, there simply did not seem to be enough hours in the day.

Not so long after Bob returned to work for Chrysler for the second time, his department was relocated from Knightsbridge to the Coventry area, a hundred miles north of London. We suddenly found ourselves packing in order to set up home with our young family in the Midlands. Our daughter Debbie was just six months old at the time.

When Bob had been working for Chrysler in Whitley, Coventry, for some time, he heard that Jensen Motors of West Bromwich were seeking a financial controller. He applied for the position and, after a couple of interviews, managed to get on a short list of three. He felt very confident and believed that God had shown him that the job was his. He was more than a little surprised and disappointed when he received a letter stating that someone else had been offered the position.

Bob was quite perturbed about this and began to doubt whether he had heard from God at all. Then two weeks later he received a phone call from the American owner of Jensen Motors, Kjell Qvale, asking Bob to go for another interview as he did not like the man that the board had chosen. The meeting went very well and Mr Qvale promptly offered Bob the job, not having the slightest notion at the time just where this appointment would lead them both.

Jensen Motors, however, was actually going into liquidation. At first it did not appear to be such a prudent move for Bob after all, as he had to lay off several hundred men and wind up the company, losing his own job as well. This would not look too good on his CV, given the fact that he was still only 27 years old. Since the task of providing for the growing needs of his family was paramount, we prayed together for God to direct us at this crucial time in our lives.

Being the entrepreneur that he was, Bob was well aware that the Jensen cars that were still on the road would need parts and servicing for a good few years to come. He used his redundancy money to set up Jensen Parts and Service in partnership with Kjell Qvale, former owner of Jensen Motors, who held the largest stake in the new company. Knowing that eventually there would be no more need for Jensen parts and servicing, Bob also managed, against all odds, to obtain the Subaru UK franchise. This would provide the platform for future growth and advancement.

Over the course of the next few years he added several other franchises to the business and was eventually able to buy out Qvale, ultimately becoming the sole shareholder. Bob continues to have a lot of respect for Kjell Qvale, and values the friendship that grew between them. He would be the first to admit with gratitude that he would almost certainly not have achieved what he has in the business world without Kjell's help, valuable advice and encouragement. Within 16 years of first joining Jensen Motors, Bob became the twenty-sixth richest man in the UK and the richest man in the Midlands.

Reaching out to all the world

Success and riches often bring problems and difficulties in their wake, but I can honestly say that at this stage Bob was, amazingly, still able to balance his spiritual, family and very full business life in an extraordinary way. He also had a wonderful relationship with each of our children, even though his work would often take him out of the country for lengthy periods.

In spite of all this worldly success, however, Bob was a frustrated man. Although highly successful as a businessman, he had always felt strongly that God had called him to be involved in missionary work of some kind. Just a few months before we married we attended a missionary meeting at a Christian conference and we both responded to a challenging appeal for young people to give a few years of their lives to work in Africa, promoting the gospel via literature. We felt at the time that this was the way God was leading, and that it was an opening for us to be involved in missions, especially as Bob had lived in Africa for some years and had a real heart to return.

We were told that we had been accepted and could go, provided Bob secured himself a job first. This should not have been a problem, as he was working for Ford at the time and it should have been fairly straightforward to get the company to agree to transfer him to the Ford Motor Company of South Africa. However, his application was rejected – twice – and we were therefore not able to go.

At the time we were very disappointed and Bob just could not understand why he was turned down when many others, much less qualified than him, were accepted. Many years later the reason became apparent. God was going to use Bob to make money, which would fund missionary work not only in Africa but in many other countries too. God's timing is certainly different from ours and His ways are beyond fathoming. We just have to put our complete trust in Him and acknowledge Him in all our ways, and, as the Bible states, 'He shall direct our paths' (Proverbs 3:6 NKJV).

Although Bob had very little money at the beginning of his working life and had to save furiously to get anything in the way of luxuries, he eventually became so wealthy that he really did not need to continue working. He was not brought up to be idle, and had in fact always enjoyed working, but there came a time in his life when he reached the conclusion that it was not worth earning money for the sake of it and he knew that he had to channel some of his wealth into the work of God. That was when he felt led by God to set up a charity called Christian Vision, giving a tenth of his corporate wealth into the venture. Christian Vision has since grown enormously and many people all over the world have been blessed, and many lives have been changed, through the charity's work. Bob's heart is mainly for evangelism by way of radio and the media, and his ultimate aim is that one billion souls are touched globally with the gospel of Jesus Christ.

The Bible tells us in 1 Peter 5:8 that the devil prowls around like a roaring lion seeking whom he may devour. He is on the lookout for those whose falling would also rock and shatter as many others as possible, causing maximum damage to individuals and relationships. The same verse also warns us to be alert, and in hindsight it is easy to see that Bob would have been a target for attack, as his testimony and wisdom were certainly recognized as a special gift from God. When our marriage reached a vulnerable stage, the devil took his opportunity to strike. The happiness and closeness that we had known as a couple, and indeed as a family, began to run through our hands like sand on a beach. And just like a stone thrown into water, our divorce would have a ripple effect on many lives.

FIVE

Come fly with me

It seemed that more and more of our time was spent on the road, travelling to and from church. Apart from putting money in the petrol companies' pockets, it did not seem to serve much of a purpose, so we decided to look for a house a little closer to where our Fellowship was located. During the process of finding a new property, however, Bob's dad tragically died in a car crash. His mum was following in another car and witnessed everything. She came to live with us for about six months, while she too hunted for a house following her husband's untimely death. It was a very traumatic time in our lives, especially as Bob's dad was only 56 when he died.

It was only after his mum was finally settled in her new home that we began hunting around again for a more suitable property ourselves. The house that we decided on was in the northern part of Coventry, and nearer the church we were attending. It stood in its own grounds in a quiet country lane, and it was a case of love at first sight for both of us the moment we saw it. It was more than we could really afford at the time, costing the princely sum of £80,000, but for that amount we were getting a six-bedroomed house, set in four acres of ground, in a picturesque former mining village called Arley, on the outskirts of Coventry. It more than met our needs in every way. It was ideally situated for Bob to get to work without travelling too far, for the children to reach their various schools easily, and for us all to attend our Fellowship.

Our new neighbours, of course, knew little or nothing about our more humble origins, and I guess most assumed that we had always enjoyed the lifestyle that was now ours. It was not that we particularly paraded our wealth – in fact, the opposite was true. Old habits die hard, and although we could now increasingly afford most things that we wanted, Bob would still delight in getting a 'two for the price of one' bargain, and I would still think twice about spending too much on clothes and would often visit the sale section to see what bargains I could pick up.

Wealth can bring its own problems. People who have very little are sometimes reluctant to invite guests to their home, because they feel embarrassed and do not want people to see the 'little' they have. At first, I have to admit, I adopted a very similar attitude – but for exactly the opposite reasons. I felt rather embarrassed, and perhaps a little guilty, about all that we now had compared to other people. After all, it was a totally different lifestyle from the kind of conditions I, or Bob for that matter, had been used to. Eventually, though, I learned to relax and enjoy the good things that God had allowed us to have. We both realized that the more we had the more we were able to give into the Kingdom of God. We also knew that everything we owned was only temporary and, as we live in a very uncertain world, could be taken from us at any time. The Bible reminds us that we are only stewards of everything that God sends and we must therefore learn to hold all our wealth very loosely indeed.

We began to realize that being a wealthy family in a normal working-class church can also have its particular problems. If a project came up where money was required, and the pastor said that the church needed to trust God for the money, we knew that some people would be wondering why Bob did not just write a cheque, solving the problem at a stroke of a pen. The same thing applied when a family had a specific financial need. We both knew, however, that first of all it was just not possible to meet every financial need within the Fellowship, and even if we could, we would end up playing God, robbing folk of exercising faith and, more seriously, turning people's eyes away from Him and on to us as the source of rescue. Having said that, we did of course help people privately from time to time as God laid them on our hearts, as any Christian couple would do. Bob's spiritual and financial advice proved to be sound, and many people valued his Godly counsel and wisdom.

Seeing the world

One of the advantages that our increased wealth brought was the ability to travel. Some very good friends of ours, Don and Pat Spicer, who attended our Fellowship and owned a shop locally, started to take holidays abroad, and more often than not we teamed up with them. We had some wonderful holidays together in Europe, and then later we tended to travel much further afield. One holiday when we were all away together was made particularly memorable as we experienced a fairly substantial earthquake.

It happened when we were in Halkadiki in Greece. We had spent a pleasant day at the beach and had wandered back to the hotel to get changed before the evening meal – except for Debbie, who decided to swim a length of the pool before going inside. From the balcony Bob decided to take a video film of her walking back to the hotel after her swim, but he could not understand why the camera was shaking so much. He thought he was having a dizzy spell. Meanwhile Andrew, who was already in his room, was fascinated to see that the mirror on the wall was swaying from side to side. None of us at that point realized that an earthquake was taking place.

The penny finally dropped when we began to hear shouts from outside the bedroom door. As we rushed out into the corridor to investigate, it seemed that everyone else on our floor had the same idea at the same time, and panic was beginning to set in. Other doors flew open and some of the (mostly German) guests, who had obviously been having showers, rushed into the corridor swathed in bath towels. Some had not bothered to cover up at all! We managed to get out of the hotel without any trouble, and waited at the gathering point until the all-clear was given several hours later. It turned out to be a fairly strong tremor, but there was only minimal structural damage and fortunately no one suffered too much harm – except perhaps a few red cheeks among the Germans!

As part of his increasing responsibilities as chairman of a large company, it was often necessary for Bob to travel to different parts of the world on business, and on occasions I was able to accompany him. The happiest times, however, were when we were able to go as a family, and we had some lovely trips to places as diverse as Spain, Malaysia, Brazil, the USA and Japan.

Another trip took us to Korea, where we visited the biggest church in the world, pastored by Dr David Yonggi Cho. Going to that church was quite an experience, and totally unlike anything we had ever encountered before, especially in England. The building holds a vast number of people, but it was still necessary to have eight services on a Sunday in order for everyone to be able to attend. Deacons of the church controlled the traffic travelling to and from the church, and inside the building there were designated areas for different nationalities, where headphones were provided so that the service could be followed in various languages. I felt really privileged to have been given the opportunity to visit this prominent and extremely fast-growing church.

It was not always possible for me to travel with Bob, because the children were at one time all at different schools and it was sometimes difficult to find friends and family members who were able to do the long school run each day. By this time, however, Bob's mum had moved to the Midlands to be near us, and on the occasions when we did travel together, she very kindly helped us as much as she could by being there for the children when they came home from school each day.

Christmas 1983 proved to be a memorable time for all the family. We had decided to visit Bob's brother Mike, who had emigrated to Australia with his wife and two young daughters the previous year. We were very glad to be able to leave the grey and cold of Britain behind for a few weeks, and head out to the sunshine and warmth of Australia. Mike and his wife Barbara were not Christians at that time and it would be true to say that, although Bob and Mike had always been very close, they did not have too much in common, as they lived very different lifestyles. In 1987, however, after they had lived in Australia for about five years, we received a telephone call one Sunday telling us that they had found the Lord and were to be baptized that afternoon. Shortly afterwards Bob was also able to lead his sister Viv to the Lord.

God had not only answered our prayers, but had also united our family in a wonderful way.

In spite of all the beautiful places we had visited, there was one place that I had wanted to go to for many years. Ever since Bob and I had first met, he had promised to take me to Kenya, where he had spent many happy years as a boy. In 1982 a holiday in Kenya was finally planned. I always knew that Bob would fulfil his promise one day, and I was excited at the prospect of visiting Africa at long last.

Our flight was due to leave London on a Sunday, and because the flight was fairly late in the day we decided to go to our church service in the morning as usual, before making our way to the airport. Obviously quite a few people knew of our travel plans, and as we sat down to await the start of the service a friend came up to us and said, 'Well, you'll not be going to Kenya then, will you.' Not having listened to the news that morning, we wondered what on earth she meant. She proceeded to explain what she had heard on the radio: there had been a military coup, and flights in and out of Kenya had been stopped. We could hardly believe our ears. In fact, we thought our friend was joking at first. It would not have been the first practical joke played on us!

It turned out to be true, however, and the annoying thing was that, had we decided to travel just 24 hours earlier, there would have been no problem as the coup would not have affected our travel plans. As it was, we now had no alternative but to reconsider our holiday plans. I could hardly believe that after all those years of waiting we had to choose the very day when it was not possible to enter the country. I wondered, at the time, if I was perhaps not meant to go to Africa after all.

We stayed in an hotel close by the airport for a day or two, to try to assess the situation, but in the end we flew to India instead, which of course was another important part of Bob's history. We did, in fact, have a lovely holiday, staying first in New Delhi, where Bob had lived as a little boy, before travelling on to Madras for a relaxing beach holiday.

The hotel we were staying at in Madras had its own beach, and each morning we would wander down to the sea shore, only to realize that, apart from one or two Indian boys a few years younger than Andrew, who was 13 at the time, we virtually had the beach to ourselves. Andrew got on well with these lads, and it did not make a scrap of difference to him that they had darker skin or that they were obviously a lot poorer than we were. All our children have been remarkably unaffected by the wealth they have known within their own surroundings, and have never looked down on people of different circumstances or ethnic groupings.

What did begin to concern Andrew, however, was the fact that each day the lads were wearing the same ragged T-shirts and shorts. It became apparent that this was all they had to wear. On the last night of our holiday, he asked if he could give the boys some of the clothes he had brought with him. After all, he would not need them once we got back to chilly Britain. We readily agreed, and he went off to find his friends and give them his parting gift. Next morning, as we were leaving the hotel, the Indian boys appeared, waving to us with big beams on their faces as they pointed to the new clothes they were proudly wearing. The biggest smile, however, was on Andrew's face, as he saw the delight that his kind deed had brought to the boys.

Andrew's concern for others actually brought another person into our family circle for a good many years. Andrew came home one day and told us about his friend Leigh, who was in his class at school and was having to leave the area because Leigh's mum had decided to move north, taking him with her. Andrew explained that Leigh did not really want to leave the area and all his friends, and as he was about 13 years old it was quite important that he stayed to finish his schooling. Andrew then hinted that if Leigh stayed with us during the week he would be able to continue his studies at the same school. Bob and I talked it over together and with our family, and finally offered to look after Leigh so that he could stay and finish his time at school. His mother agreed, and in the end Leigh remained with us until he married his wife Lynne in 1990 at the age of 21. Funnily enough, his mum never did move north, but continued to live only about a mile away for a good few years.

Although Bob and I had both felt a calling to Africa since our late teens, it was not until 1990 that I set foot on the continent for the first time. Both Andrew and Leigh were married that same year, Leigh in May and Andrew in August, and it was after these two weddings were over that we decided to try once again to visit Kenya. This time we made it – and we spent a wonderful fortnight with our two daughters, as well as Bob's mum and his sister Viv, who was by this time also a widow. It was the first time that Bob and his family had been back to Nairobi since they left in 1961, and of course it was the very first visit for myself and the girls. I did not know it at the time, but this was to be the first of many trips that I was to make to the continent of Africa.

We meet and brush shoulders with many folk in life; some we never see again, but others become a vital link in our destiny. Rob Mackenzie was one of those people. He was born in Zimbabwe but had British roots, and we first got to know him when he spent a couple of years in our church in Bedworth in the 1980s. He had been busily engaged in writing his first book and had decided to come to England in order to get the second edition published. As he was single at the time, he stayed with his mother, who happened to live in Bedworth. He very much had a heart for missionary work. He was also a talented author, and told us outrageous stories of life in Africa and of his many close shaves with wild animals.

On a later visit to England he met and married his wife Hilary. They now live in Zimbabwe and head up New Growth Ministries, looking after AIDS orphans, running a Bible course and planting churches in the African bush. As a result of meeting Rob and Hilary, Andrew and his wife Alison spent three months working with them in Africa, and Debbie also went to work with them for a few months before she married Matt. The work that Rob and Hilary do has continued to grow and God has wonderfully blessed them with a 1,000-acre farm which is being set up as a base for their ministry. They have proved to be good and faithful friends to us as a family, and although we live thousands of miles apart, the Lord has united us in His work. It is through them and their ministry that I am now involved in several missionary projects, including theirs, and consequently find myself in Africa two or three times every year.

God is so good, and when he puts a dream in your heart, it never dies. If you keep pressing on, that dream will be realized. The continent of Africa has a very special place in my heart, and I know that it touches God's heart too. 'Delight yourself in the LORD and he will give you the desires of your heart' (Psalm 37:4).

Flying high

Bob and I found that we were increasingly on guest lists to attend a growing number of social events. The company that Bob owns imports four-wheel-drive cars, and we were generally invited because he was asked to sponsor an event, or else people were looking to him for a financial donation for their good cause. We were often asked to attend top social events such as the Miss World Beauty Contest in London, the Henley Regatta and Wimbledon, as well as one or two royal garden parties.

We were also invited on several occasions to St James's Palace, where we were introduced to the Queen and Princess Margaret and on another occasion to Princess

Anne. Once we were at a function in London, waiting to go in for dinner, when the door flew open and a rather flustered Princess Diana appeared and asked someone if they knew where the loo was. She reappeared a little while later, and chatted in a very relaxed way to the group of people nearest to her. Although I did not speak to her myself, I was struck with how tall she was, compared to Princess Margaret who was much smaller than I had imagined her to be.

When I first started to go to functions of this kind, I felt very much out of my depth and spoke very little, for fear of saying the wrong thing. Nonetheless, although the surroundings and situations were far removed from anything I had been used to in earlier times, I never felt particularly overawed by the many top businessmen and their wives whom I met. In fact, I sometimes felt sorry for some of them, as the shallowness of their lives was highlighted in the conversations they had with each other. I longed to tell them that their spiritual condition was something of much greater importance than two women wearing a similar dress at the same dinner party, but at the time I felt it wiser to bite my tongue and say nothing! Perhaps, however, these were missed opportunities when I should have spoken up for the Lord but never did.

In view of all the high-society functions we were now attending, including many equestrian events, which could be anywhere in the country, Bob decided that he would like to learn to fly so that he could get around more easily and certainly a lot more quickly. Flying was in his blood, given that his dad had been a professional pilot during Bob's formative years. In 1980, Bob decided that the time was now right for him to follow in his father's footsteps. He joined the flying school at Kidlington Airport near Oxford, took an intensive course, and before long had got his private pilot's licence and could fly anywhere he wanted to, either on his own or with the family.

As Bob had learned to fly outside the Coventry area, I had never seen him at the controls of an aeroplane before and was therefore very nervous the first few times that I went up with him. I wanted to appear relaxed, but became increasingly aware that I was almost twisting my fingers off my hands in fear, at the same time praying that he would be able to get us all back safely to solid ground – especially when we had the children with us. Bob had bought a Fuji semi-aerobatic single-engine aeroplane. It was a four-seater, built like a tank, with metal switches, but it was a very stable aircraft and as time went on, I gradually began to relax as I accepted the fact that Bob was a qualified pilot and did perhaps know what he was doing after all.

I could never have guessed, however, that he was planning to 'treat' me to flying lessons for my thirty-eighth birthday! I could hardly believe my ears when he rang me from the office one morning to say that he had booked me some flying lessons as a birthday present. 'I thought birthday gifts were supposed to be something to be *enjoyed*!' I said. 'I'm really not sure what to say – but thanks anyway . . .'

I then thought that I would try to rise to the challenge. At least I might be able to learn the basics so that I could cope if an emergency should ever occur. I really only intended to have a couple of lessons, but found that this new 'sport' got right into my blood. I soon found myself flying above the clouds with my instructor during the day, and trying to sort out the mysteries of bearings and dead reckonings in the evenings – all of which had to be mastered if I was to become a fully qualified pilot. My lack of expertise in maths once more became painfully apparent, but I persevered.

I also had to go through the nerve-racking experience of flying totally alone for the first time. I was going out with my instructor as usual, but just as we were about to taxi onto the runway he suddenly announced that he was deserting me: I was about to do my first solo flight. He promptly left me sitting alone in the plane, with no other option but to take off. He must have had faith that I could return his beloved aeroplane to him in one piece, as he reassured me that everything was going to be fine, and that he would talk me through every move from the control tower. With my heart in my mouth, I started to 'roll' and soon I was flying solo for the first time – quite a milestone in any pilot's life.

The instructor obviously knew more about my abilities than I did. I completed the circuit and landed with no problems. Eventually, after many months, I also became the proud holder of a private pilot's licence and it was not long before I was well and truly bitten by the flying bug. I began to love taking the controls of an aircraft almost as much as Bob did. I rarely flew alone, however, and I once proudly flew all the family to the Isle of Wight.

One day, a close friend who had heard that I had learned to fly asked me, half joking, if I would take him up for a spin. I agreed – much to his horror. To be fair to him, although he was terrified of heights, he did turn up on the appointed day for his 'flight of a lifetime'. Unfortunately, the poor chap had worked himself up into such a state that he was sick before the plane even left the hangar. I have never found out whether it was the thought of me at the controls or his tangible fear of heights that made him throw up. He was very courageous, though, and did stay aboard until the flight was complete. I am very pleased to report that he lived to tell the tale.

I have to be honest about one thing, though: navigation was not my strongest point. One day, while I was out flying with a friend of mine who had also gained her wings but did not have much chance to fly, we thought we were flying over Staverton in Gloucestershire. We radioed Staverton Airport asking their permission to land, which was promptly given. Then, much to our dismay, we suddenly spotted the Clifton Suspension Bridge, near Bristol. Somehow or other we had got our bearings terribly wrong. We hurriedly turned the aircraft round and looked out for some landmarks. We ended up following the River Severn until we spotted the famous Worcester Cathedral, and then turned right towards Coventry Airport. Miraculously, and due to no skill on our part, we ended up exactly on course. Maybe my navigation was not so bad after all! In recent years, however, I reluctantly took the decision to let my licence lapse. In the end I was only flying in order to keep my licence current. My flying days were such fun while they lasted, though.

Stewards of wealth

Money can solve all kinds of problems, of course, and we knew ourselves to be very fortunate to have no worries about income. Wealth is not a solution to everything, however, and indeed brings with it a whole new set of responsibilities and even vulnerabilities. Our own wealth, for example, brought us into the public eye in a way that was not always welcome. Bob was often referred to in the local paper as 'the Arley millionaire' – something that in the end he took steps to prevent. We also began to realize that an increasing number of people knew who we were, with our respective cars recognized in the locality, although we had no idea at all who *they* were.

Knowing that greed and envy can do strange things to some people, we always made sure that we picked up the children from wherever they were, rather than letting them make their own way home. We did not make a big thing about it, but we felt it wise to be cautious. We also took precautions to have the house protected, and varied our comings and goings so that we had no set pattern that people could predict. We knew that God was very much in control of our lives and that He would protect us, but at the same time we believed that He also expects us to be wise in these matters and not take unnecessary chances.

There were also many begging letters to contend with – something that most people who are in the public eye seem to receive. A large proportion of them were obviously just standard letters that people would send to anyone they thought might give them something for nothing, and these normally ended up in the waste bin. We even had some 'long-lost' relatives make contact with us, some with exotic names, of whom no one in the family had ever heard! We tended to reply to begging letters with our own standard letter, saying that we supported a range of charities – which was true – which took up the money we had allocated to good causes.

The time eventually arrived when we both felt that we would like either to move or to extend and alter our present house. Although still very homely and comfortable, the house was now in need of a certain amount of tender loving care and, with the children quickly growing into adults (with the addition of Leigh, of course, we had four children at home), it would be good if they could have some extra space for themselves and maybe somewhere to entertain their friends.

We started to look around for a bigger house to buy in the area, but after seeing what was on offer we decided that there was absolutely nothing to match our own home anywhere on the market. Over the years, as the farmland surrounding the house had gradually become available, we had purchased it. Our property now stood in 14 acres, and we owned all the land right up to the railway line in one direction, as well as the land up to the nearest house in the other direction – a house which ultimately Andrew and his wife Alison would buy.

We decided that altering and enlarging the house was the right way to go. After the plans for the extension had been passed, Bob went to work designing the new layout, while I began to put together some ideas for the decor. Bob wanted a big lounge area – and when I say big, I really do mean big. He also liked straight walls, with no nooks and crannies or odd corners. For my part, I wanted something stylish but very cosy and homely. I left most of the main planning to Bob and the architect, but insisted on putting my touch to one or two of the rooms, especially the bedrooms.

The preparation work was started at the end of 1988 and the building was finally completed in 1991, enormously increasing the value of our original property. As with everything that we had, however, we tried to hold it loosely, and also to share it with as many people as we could, while at the same time using it for the Lord's work as appropriate. After all, one of the joys of being blessed with nice things is being able to share them with others. I was very pleased with the end result. Although it meant dust and disruption for longer than I care to remember, so many people have commented on the lovely atmosphere within the house, which is something that all the money in the world cannot create.

Lovely as all these material things were and are, however, I was always acutely aware that having plenty of money does have its drawbacks. Children, for instance, can so easily take things for granted. I am glad to say that this has not been the case as far as our own children are concerned. When people come into wealth suddenly, it can cause them to go off balance and do the craziest things. The Bible says that it is hard for a rich man to enter the Kingdom of God, and I know that to be true. It is hard – but, of course, it is not impossible. Sometimes people misquote the Bible and say that money is the root of all evil, but what the Bible actually says is this: 'For the love of money is a root of all kinds of evil. Some people, eager for money, have wandered from the faith and pierced themselves with many griefs' (1 Timothy 6:10). Wealth is not bad, it is the lust and wrong use of it that is unhealthy.

By the time 1991 had come and gone, I had a highly successful and wealthy husband, three wonderful children and a daughter-in-law, all of whom I loved to bits, a big involvement in a thriving church, a lovely house, many good friends and, to crown it all, I knew without a shadow of a doubt that God loved me and that I had a wonderful destiny to fulfil. God was my Heavenly Father and I knew He wanted to fill my life with many good things. I knew He wanted to bless me even more than He had done already. What an awesome God we serve.

Yet lurking in the background was a situation which was growing increasingly serious by the day, and which would eventually end up tearing Bob and me apart. Sadly, I was just not spiritually wise enough at that time to recognize it or, in fact, to be able to deal with it in the way the Word of God instructs us to – even though I had been a Christian since I was 10 years old.

SIX

I will build my church

We stayed at the first church we had joined in the Coventry area, Keresley Pentecostal Church, for about four years. Eventually, however, we began to feel that God was speaking to us, and a small group of others within the Fellowship, about branching out into a neighbouring town and starting work there. A bit like Abraham, who was called by God to move from his familiar surroundings, we left the Keresley church in the mid-1970s, not quite knowing what was in store for us but with a firm conviction that the Lord was definitely leading us to pastures new.

Not everyone was in total agreement with our decision to move on, however.

When God calls people to move on in this way, it can sometimes be a time of real blessing and excitement, but at the same time it can be very difficult as people leave behind what has been familiar to them for years and go off into a completely new and unknown situation. As Bob and I had not been at Keresley for too many years, it was no truly great wrench for us – but for some who moved with us, the church had been their spiritual home since childhood and they left with very mixed feelings. Who can say why God moved us all on in the way that He did, other than that He wanted a Christian witness in the Bedworth area, and He saw that this particular town was ready for what He wanted to do. Interestingly enough, all those who moved with us to Bedworth at that time are still involved in the Lord's work in one way or another.

Small beginnings

There were about 16 adults and an assortment of children, ranging from toddlers to early teens, who formed the new church. I am not being unduly modest when I say that none of us was particularly gifted or blessed in any area which indicated that God would use any of us to pastor a church that would eventually grow much bigger than we envisaged, becoming one of the strongest churches in the Assemblies of God movement, and indeed within the Midlands. We were just very ordinary people. Apart from Bob and myself and our three children, there were about four other couples and their children. Two of the couples have already been mentioned – Ralph Coleman and his wife Gill and, of course, our friends Don and Pat Spicer and their two children. A few singles made up the rest of the number.

We were all aware that some other Christians, encouraged by the Assemblies of God Home Missions Department, had started to meet in Bedworth some years earlier. Sadly, it seemed that the timing of that particular church planting was obviously not right, for the work never really flourished and eventually had to be closed down. We also heard that the previous group had left a rather shabby caravan behind, which rotted, giving the locals a daily reminder for some time afterwards of the 'Pentecostals' who had been in their midst. We therefore had a few metaphorical fences to mend when we started to hold regular services in the area several years later.

We looked for a suitable building in which we could meet each week, and managed to find a primary school on the outskirts of Bedworth that we were able to rent for a limited period of time. This gave us the opportunity to look around for something a little more permanent, while we got the work underway in the meantime.

It did not take us too long to find a suitable permanent site. The Old Hob Lane School, as it was then called, was right in the centre of Bedworth and had been empty for some time. After looking round it and realizing that the location was excellent, even though the building was in a bad state of repair, we decided to purchase it. It was frankly nothing to write home about, having been severely neglected, and the whole place needed a good bit of work before we felt we had got it to a reasonable standard.

As soon as the mortgage had been arranged and the building was officially ours, we moved in and were relieved of paying rent each week at the primary school. Before we could do anything as basic as painting the walls, however, we had to rid the inside of the building of the plant life that had managed to take root! Everyone worked very hard, and soon we had a meeting place of which we could all be proud. Now we had a base in the very centre of Bedworth where we could worship God and invite others to do the same. It was not a large building. It had one main room and another smaller room at the back which we used for the Sunday School. It also had a small kitchen where we made coffee and tea after the Sunday evening service. We found that the times spent relating together were just as important as the times we spent worshipping God, and we soon grew together as a close team.

I will never forget the first meeting we held there shortly after the building officially became ours. It was a rather chilly day, and in order to keep warm we lit a fire in the small room at the back, forgetting that corrugated iron was still covering the windows. Many of the windows had been broken, so we needed them covered until the glass was replaced, as vandalism was a real problem in the area. It meant, however, that there was nowhere for the smoke to escape to, which left us all coughing and spluttering. After a very brief time of praise and worship, we beat a hasty retreat! We were, at the same time, very grateful to God for His goodness in providing us with a building of our own in which we could meet together regularly.

Prayer for a pastor

The men all knew that they were not called to pastor the church, but they were willing to pull their weight, work together as a team and support the work in any way they could, which was exactly what was required in such a small fellowship. We all felt that pastoring a church was a definite calling and, if God had led us this far, He would certainly provide us with the man of His choice who would be able to build the church and pastor the folk who would eventually join us. In the meantime they were all quite willing to take their turn at preaching each Sunday if necessary – although the Assemblies of God Home Missions Department were very good in supplying preachers, so their services were not called upon too often.

We had a couple of false starts as far as choosing a pastor was concerned. On two separate occasions we thought we had the right man, only for circumstances to prove otherwise. We therefore began to make it a special matter of prayer that the man God had chosen would be revealed. Just a little while later, one of the young men connected to our former church in Keresley, who was also a personal friend of ours, came on the phone to speak to Bob about something. His name was John Partington – a slim, fair-haired fellow with a real pioneering spirit, who had spent some time at Bible college before pastoring a church on the Isle of Wight with his wife Andrene.

'How's the new church coming along?' said John after he had talked through the business he had with Bob.

'Fine, just fine,' Bob replied.

'Got yourselves a pastor yet?' was John's next question.

'Funny you should say that,' said Bob, half joking, 'because we're praying for one right now. In fact, we've been praying for a tall, fair-haired chap who is currently living in the Isle of Wight . . .'

'Is that so?' said John, sounding more than a little interested. 'Well, I'd need to pray about it, of course, but it would at least be good to come over sometime and chat a little more about things.'

The rest of the story, as they say, is history. After much discussion and prayer, John Partington, supported by his wife, became the pastor of the newly formed Bedworth Pentecostal Church, as it was initially called. Their induction service took place in June 1976. The day is vividly etched in my memory as being the hottest day of the year, with temperatures soaring into the 90s and the small back hall, which was the first room to be completed, packed to capacity. In spite of the unbearable heat, it was a day of great blessing as people from far and near joined in the service of dedication.

The church was now able to move forward and get involved in reaching out to the community in which we lived. It did, however, become clear before too long that the church needed some sort of structure. John was our pastor and from day one we knew that he was sent to us by God, but he now needed to think about appointing elders or deacons to help him. John decided that he would appoint just one elder initially, in whom he could confide as far as spiritual and church matters were concerned.

Up to this time, the men in the Fellowship had formed a temporary deaconate and had to make most of the decisions themselves, some of them major. They were all in agreement that an elder should be appointed to help carry some of the spiritual load. Bob was the man John recommended as the first elder of the church. He was a few years older than John, and they got on very well together. John found it easy to talk to Bob about a range of things, and Bob enjoyed John's company too. The rest of the Fellowship were happy about the choice, and so Bob began to assume more responsibilities in the church – just as his job also became more demanding. Yet he took his responsibilities as an elder very seriously, and people soon began to realize that the advice he gave them, both spiritual and secular, was good and sound. As an elder's wife, I was sometimes called upon when a couple needed help. We prayed together regularly for the health of the church, and that souls in the town of Bedworth would be saved.

Active growth

The church held two services on a Sunday, morning and evening, and we also ran a Sunday School, as well as holding mid-week meetings. Our heart's desire as a church was that those living in our area might experience the love and saving power of Jesus Christ, as we had all done. We also began to participate in a range of activities that would draw others into the church – and, more importantly, would draw others into a relationship with Jesus. Apart from various outreach meetings, when we would invite a speaker to come along, we posted Scripture tracts through letterboxes, invited our workmates to the activities at the church, and did whatever else we could to reach the many needs of the people around us.

Bob and I were both involved with the musical side of things, too. Bob had his guitar, of course, and I played the piano at several of the meetings. We took the children along from a very early age, and they simply accepted that church was where we would be every Sunday. Bob and I took it in turns to attend the weeknight services. The services were lively and happy occasions, with hymns and choruses that we all enjoyed and that particularly emphasized biblical truths. Every member of the church was active and lent a helping hand with the menial tasks such as making tea or coffee, washing up and cleaning the toilets. We believed strongly as a Fellowship that every Christian should aspire to adopt a serving attitude towards others and towards God.

God began to bless the work at Bedworth, and all our hard work and the faithfulness of the church members began to be rewarded. John was a real visionary and pastored the church extremely well. Whole families started to be added, slowly but consistently. Things eventually reached the point where people had to arrive at church early to get a good seat. The mid-week meetings were also well attended. Tuesday evening was our prayer meeting, and Thursday was the evening we put aside to study the Bible. As more and more people began to come along, we started to wonder just how long it would be before we needed to look around for a bigger building.

At the beginning of the 1980s we split our mid-week meetings into housegroups rather than continuing to hold one large meeting. It was felt that closer ties could be formed when a small group of people met on a regular basis, and it also allowed more people to open up and join in with the spiritual discussion. Some of us were a little wary of the housegroup idea at first, but it seemed to work well, and the church continued to grow at a fairly fast pace.

Bob and I had a good relationship with all those who came along to the church, but the Spicer family were the ones we bonded with the most. Bob and Don got on extremely well, and Pat and I also hit it off right from the very first time we met. Although we did not live in each other's pockets and rarely sat together in church, we would often go round to each other's houses for supper on a Sunday night after church, and we very often spent our summer holidays together. They had two children at the time, and little did I know as the years rolled on that both children would have a considerable impact upon us as a family, in totally different ways. It is undoubtedly for the best that none of us knows everything that the future holds.

After about 10 years, when the church was continuing to grow above all expectations, another milestone was reached. It became obvious that we could no longer use our renovated school building for the Sunday services – it had become far too small. We started to meet each Sunday at a local comprehensive school, while still holding our weeknight services in the church. We knew this could only be a temporary arrangement, however, and it was clearly not the answer to the problem.

What we really needed to do was to construct a purpose-built church of our own. After many weeks of prayer and discussion, we suddenly found ourselves in the midst of a massive project to build a new 500-seater church with offices and crèche facilities, designed in such a way that it could cope with any further growth in the years to come. Bob was once again heavily involved in that project, while the rest of the church rallied round to raise the funds necessary to embark on such an exciting venture.

SEVEN

Building a people of power

Although Bob was the first elder to be appointed, others including Don Spicer and Ralph Coleman were later also made elders as the church began to grow. They started to pray with John Partington about how they could best accommodate the increasing number of people now coming to the church on a regular basis. It was a wonderful 'problem' to have, but one that had to be addressed with a certain amount of urgency.

Once it had been decided that the solution was to construct a new church building from scratch,

Bob used his business knowledge and his many contacts to form a construction team that could carry out the work. A huge amount of money – around £800,000 – had to be raised for the project. An appropriate piece of land also had to be found and purchased, and plans drawn up and approved by the local authority. We all began to realize at this stage what a mammoth task lay ahead of us.

The larger school premises we had moved into were fine and more than adequately accommodated us, but it meant putting out chairs for every service that was held there, as well as bringing along everything we needed, like musical instruments, a projector for the words of the choruses we sang, and all the material needed to run the Sunday School. It also meant, of course, that some of us had to get there well ahead of the start of the service, and then others had to stay behind afterwards to put everything away. This was not the first time I had been in a church where this procedure had gone on. In fact, it seemed to be a recurring feature in the churches I had been involved with in the past. The Fellowship in Elm Park had met in a hired hall, bringing in everything we needed for the service each week. Then, after we left the first church we had joined in Coventry in order to establish a Fellowship in Bedworth, we had hired a primary school for a short time before we bought the old Hob Lane School, and once again everything we needed for each service had to be fetched and carried.

Our children, who had been quite small when we started at the church, were by this time fast growing into adults, as were the rest of their friends, and the young people of the church were as active in the development of the church as their parents. Don's and Pat's son Gary, for example, had taken a job in a shop after he had left school, although he had felt God's call on his life since the age of 14. When Gary was about 19, John noticed his potential and asked him to take responsibility for the young people of the church. Gary became the church's official youth leader. This was not a full-time appointment as is generally the custom today, but Gary managed to build up the youth group in a phenomenal way, as well as keeping his job going at the shop.

The church was bursting at the seams, and the news that a suitable piece of land was for sale did not come a moment too soon. We decided to put in a bid. The land in which we were interested had at one time had a factory on it, with residential property close by. Now it seemed that half the street was being demolished for redevelopment purposes, and the rest of the land lay idle. Nonetheless, the question of how we were going to pay for the land and the subsequent building weighed heavily on everyone's mind. John challenged the church members by reminding them that it was not just another church project, but a means by which many in the area would come to understand and experience God's love in their lives. Many caught the vision, and pledges started to come in. A building fund was opened and the church was able to negotiate for the land, and draw up plans for the building itself.

Meanwhile, our links with other Christian fellowships in the area were growing. The local Baptist minister would sometimes take our morning service, while John took the service at the Baptist church. The United Reformed church was also very close by, and sometimes we used their building for different functions, which all helped to build up relationships within the Christian community.

The building programme drew our own church together in a new way. Now, apart from our primary task of introducing people to Jesus, we were also involved in praying for the new building as it went through the planning stages and then finally began to take shape before our eyes. It had been cleverly designed so that one wall could be 'pushed out' if future growth demanded that the building be made larger. We had experienced steady growth already, but we believed that this was something God wanted to continue, and we therefore had to be prepared for it.

I have to admit that I no longer knew the names of all the people who now came to the church. I recognized most by sight, but it was virtually impossible to get to know everyone in the way we had done at the beginning. The housegroups helped in some ways, but it meant that the whole church was now only together on a Sunday, which is not always the best time to get to know people better.

A change of pastor

Just as we were all ready to move into our lovely new building, our pastor dropped a bombshell. John announced one day that he felt God was calling him to pioneer another fellowship – an inner-city church in Liverpool, at least two hours' drive further north. It seemed strange in a way that he had been our pastor all through the difficult times of building up the numbers, and then enthusing everyone about the new church building, only to move on just as things would inevitably get a little easier for him. But John was a pioneer at heart, and before he got too comfortable, I believe God moved him on to a new field of work. (Maybe this is the point when I should let you into a little secret: the close friend who very bravely came for a spin in the single-engine aeroplane with me was none other than our dear pastor, John Partington. I would like to think that this incident had nothing to do with his sudden move to Liverpool!)

After the initial shock of realizing that John would soon no longer be our pastor, the big question was, who would fill the gap left by John and his family? By this time Gary Spicer had been appointed as the youth pastor, helped by his wife Helen. Meanwhile, the elders of the church started to discuss and pray about who should replace John. After some time they felt it right to approach someone they all knew quite well and reckoned would be good for the future health of the church. To their delight, when the idea was put to that person, he too felt positive about the whole idea. During the time that he was considering the proposal, however, he died very suddenly. Shocked and grieved, we were thrown into a quandary. Had we, in fact, heard from God at all? But God showed us very clearly that He had chosen another man.

A second man was considered and approached, who also felt positive about the idea of becoming our next pastor, but before anything was finalized we heard that he had left his church very suddenly, under a bit of a cloud. By this time John had started at his new church in Liverpool, but he had agreed to remain in fellowship with the leaders of our church until a new pastor was appointed. It was finally decided by the elders to take a completely different approach. They wanted to hear from God and have His choice, and so they asked John for his prayerful input into the decision concerning his successor.

About three weeks later and after several discussions with the leadership, John rang Gary Spicer quite late one evening and asked if they could meet. Gary drove to a motorway café between Coventry and Liverpool, and he and John chatted deep into the night. Gary had no idea why he was there, or why he was being asked so many questions. Finally, after a few hours of intense talk, John suddenly wound up the conversation by saying, 'Gary, you're the man to replace me.'

It was a massive shock for Gary. He drove home, wondering what reaction Helen would have. As it happened, she was as shocked as he was. Neither of them quite believed at the time that they were suitably equipped to take on the pastorate of such a fast-growing, influential church. However, after much prayer and heart-searching, and in spite of the fact that they felt very inexperienced and perhaps a little inadequate, they both had the assurance that God was calling them into full-time service at Bedworth, and they both knew that He would equip them for the task that lay ahead. Thus Gary became our new pastor at the tender age of 26.

Understandably, it took some people a little while to get used to the idea. After all, some of us, including Bob and I, had known him since he was a lad. A few inevitably left the church when John went to Liverpool, but the majority recognized the special giftings that God had put within Gary, and felt that making him our next pastor was certainly the right move. We knew that, although the youth group had grown in leaps and bounds, being youth pastor had not exactly been a piece of cake for Gary, and yet he had been faithful, and had shown that he wanted to learn from all the experiences he had been through.

A thriving fellowship

No sooner had we said our final goodbye to John and Andrene and their three children, than we were moving into our new church. The new building was throbbing with life, with lots going on for all age groups, attracting even more people and making me feel that I would never remember all their names! The church was in a good location on a main road, with houses nearby, which all contributed to its healthy development. Later we were to open a restaurant and a crèche, and would eventually buy two neighbouring houses to give us more room for the work that was taking place at the church.

The Lord really began to bless Gary and the church in a mighty way. John had been a pioneer, whereas Gary was someone who was able to establish what John had introduced. He was not afraid of standing up for what he felt was right, even with people much older than himself. This was an attribute that would be tested many times, and particularly as my own traumatic circumstances unfolded.

Celebration-type services became a hallmark of the Fellowship, with plenty of music and lively preaching with an emphasis on the Word, and services lasting easily up to two hours. Church is not a unit in isolation, but is made up of individuals within a community. One of our aims was to meet those people and minister to them where they were, and by doing that we became very involved with the local people. Yet the work in which the church started to get involved became much bigger than the small number of founder members could ever have imagined. Our Family Centre was recognized by social services for the sacrificial work that was being done with pre-school children, as well as with the youth of the area, and also in the mothers' and toddlers' group. The church also started to work, in conjunction with social services, with children from underprivileged families, taking them on holiday each year and making sure that each family had adequate food and at least one gift for each child at Christmas.

Gary and Helen have an ongoing vision for the church, desiring to impact areas of the community that traditionally have been hard ground for Christians in the past. They know there are many people in the surrounding area who desperately need to experience the love of God, but for a multitude of reasons would never dream of visiting a church, except for weddings and funerals. It is also their desire to release members of the church to go out where the people are, and show the love of God to them in a range of practical ways. Helen is especially sensitive to the needs of women, not only from the community but also further afield, and she has a burning desire to see them released from the failures, mistakes and hurts of the past, into all the wonderful things that God has promised them.

It is generally accepted that church numbers are declining in Britain, and sadly that is true in many instances where worship of God has become formal and remote from everyday life. Yet where the power of the Holy Spirit is allowed to operate, and where the good news of Jesus is preached, with signs following and emphasis on biblical truths, the situation is completely different. That kind of church is growing steadily week by week, as people's lives are changed and they come into contact with the risen Lord. It affects every part of their life – the way they think, the way they relate to others, the way they give. It is nothing short of a revolutionary change, and it is happening to hundreds of thousands of people in Great Britain today.

We give God all the glory for the great things He has done and is going to do in Bedworth – not only in terms of numbers, but in the lives of those who attend the church. It is our desire to see lives changed and many bondages broken as the Word of God is allowed to penetrate and completely revolutionize lives. We serve an awesome God.

EIGHT

Breaking up
is hard to do

In the same way that our Fellowship was growing and prospering, so Bob's business career was on the upward spiral too. And, as Bob moved higher up the career ladder, I confess that I found it difficult to accept the fact that he gave both personal and business work to his secretaries. He tended to give them all the nitty-gritty details he did not want to be bothered with, which often included private family matters. It took me a while to get used to the fact that there were others who were so close to him.

I knew that it was vital for a man in Bob's position to have personal assistants to help him function efficiently, and I eventually accepted that they were a necessary part of his life. In fact, I became grateful to them, as Bob's life was made so much easier by their efficiency and professionalism that he was able to spend more time with us as a family. Yet in every relationship there are social and interpersonal boundaries that should never be crossed. This is true with everyone to whom we relate, be it the window cleaner, the door-to-door salesman or even the bank manager. Obviously different rules apply, depending on how well the person concerned is known, and on what basis the relationship operates. I believe, however, that lines have to be drawn in order for any relationship to serve its intended purpose, and once those perimeters are violated, havoc is potentially unleashed. I am not saying that this always happens, but it certainly opens the door wide for relationship breakdown.

When we allow perimeters and boundaries to be invaded, we invite destruction into our lives in the same way that an insecure home is an invitation to a burglar to come and violate it. Of course, to rob and steal is wrong, but knowing that people who do these things exist, we take every care to secure our homes with all the latest locking systems and burglar alarms, to make sure that it is totally safe and very difficult for a thief to break in and steal our goods. Why is it, then, that we do not do the same with our lives? As Christians we know that Satan our enemy is there, waiting to rob, kill and destroy, so why do we open the door, making it easy for him to have his way?

I am sure that the age-old boss/secretary relationship scenario must have begun by stepping over relationship thresholds that are out of bounds, probably through home and personal life overlapping with business. It is surely important, therefore, that both boss and secretary have carefully defined boundaries within which they operate, so that their working relationship can function properly and in an orderly way.

Bob had previously had several secretaries where this good principle worked perfectly, but when he decided to employ the daughter of our friends, someone whom we had both known since she was eight years old, I felt uneasy in my spirit about it and talked it over with Bob on several occasions. She was an efficient worker and an asset to Bob in his daily routine, but I felt that, because of her already close links with the family and involvement with the church, her appointment as Bob's PA would not be a particularly wise move and could cause many complications on both sides.

There were numerous occasions in the years that followed when I felt strongly that my initial instincts had not been far wrong, but as the topic became something of a sore point in the home, I chose to say nothing. I felt that if I did pursue it, and Bob consequently changed his secretary, it would be held against me should he end up with someone less efficient. I seemed to be in a no-win situation.

Peacemaker or peacekeeper?

In hindsight I believe that I was totally deceived into thinking I was being what the Bible calls a 'peacemaker'.

I kept the peace by letting things ride and by turning a blind eye to matters that should have been faced up to and discussed. At the same time, however, I often thought that perhaps there was no substance to my fears and I was simply being paranoid and silly. Nonetheless, what my instincts told me was ultimately confirmed, as they married only two months after the divorce was made absolute.

Often our flesh will tell us one thing when actually the opposite is the real truth. I believe there is a difference between being a peacemaker and being a peacekeeper. I was being a peacekeeper. 'Anything for a quiet life' was my attitude, when I should have been facing up to the situation and not just hoping that it would go away all by itself. I was being passive, and I have come to believe that passivity is a highly dangerous thing. Being a peace*maker* means that sometimes we have to confront and deal with painful matters in our own life and maybe in the lives of those close to us, in order to resolve the problem and bring peace and harmony into the situation. It does not mean putting our head in the sand like an ostrich in the hope that the situation will somehow change.

I believe that sometimes we are reluctant to confront a situation because we are scared of the truth about ourselves, not the other person. We should never turn a blind eye to things that we know are wrong and do not line up with what the Word of God says. The Bible says, 'Blessed are the peacemakers' (Matthew 5:9), and if we want to be truly blessed we must strive to be peacemakers, in a loving way, and not just peacekeepers. The devil loves to distort the truth and keep us in darkness and confusion. Yet we are not called to live by what *seems* right, but by what *is* right. The truth will undoubtedly set us free, but unfortunately the truth is not always comfortable. Sometimes we run away from the very things that are able to set us free and bring release and freedom into our lives. Refusing to confront and deal with these issues will not resolve the problem, as the root still remains and will continue to grow, causing bigger and bigger problems.

Jesus wants to heal our wounds and set us absolutely and totally free, but we often prefer to take a much easier and more convenient road, because to humble ourselves and let God deal with us His way speaks of discipline and maybe even the shelving of our own desires and aspirations. We need to choose to allow God to prune us and cut back all those undesirable pieces of unwanted growth that prevent us from coming into God's fullness and hinder our Christian walk, in order that we might have the quality of life our Heavenly Father desires us to have.

It is my prayer as you read this book that God will give you a burning desire to be free from the bondages, rejections and setbacks of the past and that, whatever happens to you in life, you are able to deal with those problems in a victorious way, recognizing what is really happening and who your real enemy is. The Bible says, 'Let us lay aside every weight, and the sin that so easily ensnares us, and let us run with endurance the race that is set before us' (Hebrews 12:1 NKJV).

If we allow boundaries in our lives to be violated and hurts and wounds from the past, perhaps going back as far as our childhood, to keep us in bondage, we invite strife into our lives and we will not be able to enjoy the freedom and abundant life that Jesus died to give us. 'Where there is strife there is every evil work' (James 3:16 NKJV).

Learning to forgive

One of the keys, I believe, is forgiveness. There is that word again, the one we all love to hate. The whole concept of forgiveness is often spoken about by Jesus – but when it begins to be an undeniable issue in our own lives, due to circumstances that have been forced upon us, it becomes something that we are unable to deal with without God's help. I know that forgiveness certainly does not happen overnight. It is a journey that has to be walked – and if, immediately after someone has tried to destroy you or someone close to you, you say that you have totally forgiven them, you are probably in denial, because forgiveness is a *process*. It can certainly be speeded up, however, and you can save yourself a lot of heartache and pain if you choose to walk down the road that leads to forgiveness from the very outset. Eventually you will be able to say truthfully that you have forgiven that person, because you have exposed yourself to God's healing process rather than letting the actions of those who have wounded or wronged you so badly bring corrosion and decay to every area of your life.

I thought that I had always been able to forgive fairly easily, as it was not something that had ever given me too much trouble in the past – until my marriage ran into difficulties. That traumatic situation threw me totally, and I realized that forgiveness is not so easy after all. In fact, at one time I thought it to be a total impossibility. But let me tell you one thing that really helped me to put my feet on the path of forgiveness. I was praying one day, and the Lord reminded me that none of us was dealing with flesh and blood, but with principalities and powers of darkness.

It certainly did feel a dark situation. It seemed at one stage that absolutely everything was working against me, and it was only then that I realized I should be directing my anger at the devil, the father of lies, and not at individual personalities. They too were victims of Satan's evil plots and devices. I began to pray in a different manner as I realized that I too had been totally deceived. I needed to repent of any wrongs on my part, being ignorant of the devil's schemes, and of neglecting to acknowledge God in all my ways. I asked the Lord to forgive me and to begin to reveal the truths of His Word to me so that I could become the whole person He desired me to be.

The Bible says that we should not be ignorant of the devil's devices. When you are in a battle, you have to understand warfare tactics, or you will be picked off by the enemy. The good news for Christians is that the battle is already won, the devil is a defeated foe and all we have to do is to walk the way God tells us to and avail ourselves of the weapons of warfare that He has lovingly provided for us.

The blood of Jesus is powerful and victorious, and is able to cleanse us and protect us from all evil. He has also given us His Word, which is quick and powerful, sharper than any two-edged sword, never returns to Him void and always accomplishes the task it was sent to do. There is such power and authority in the name of Jesus. We cannot lose if we keep our eyes on Him and learn how to overcome all the fiery darts of the enemy. As the Bible reminds us, 'Greater is he that is in you than he that is in the world' (1 John 4:4 KJV).

As Christians, we have the living Word and also the whole armour of God at our disposal. All we have to do is put it on. Spiritual warfare is not just casting out demons by the laying on of hands. It is walking in love, when all around is hate. It is praising God when everything around us appears dark and there seems to be no way out. It is also forgiving when our circumstances dictate that revenge would be a better solution. I believe that revenge is not sweet to a child of God. And when we act according to the Scriptures and the blueprint that the Lord lays down, demons have to flee. They cannot stay around when God is praised regardless of our circumstances.

'I hate divorce,' says God

Marriage is under threat all over the world like never before, and no one is immune. Divorce is now as prevalent in church circles as it is in the world. We may justify our actions by saying, 'Well, it happens all the time, it's the days we live in – everybody does it!' That does not make it right, even if you believe it, because God's precepts have not changed. The Bible reads the same as it did hundreds of years ago, and the message has not altered one bit. God's way is perfect, and you cannot improve on perfection. The Bible tells us that God hates divorce (Malachi 2:16), and that is the truth. He hates it because it falls outside the pattern that He has laid down for His children, and because of the mayhem it causes to close-knit families and the destruction it can bring to many individuals, as well as the effect it has on society.

I believe that many men and women, and spiritual leaders too, have missed their true destiny and found themselves on a totally different path in life because of their decision to divorce the one whom they think is the cause of all their problems – when in fact their marriage partner is probably the very person that they need, the person whom the Lord put beside them to enrich their lives in a special way. We should constantly remind ourselves that the devil is a liar.

The real truth is that many people in that situation probably have a number of things festering inside, maybe from past hurts or childhood abuses, or they may be struggling with character problems within themselves, and their inner turmoil may not be anything to do with the marriage at all. Yet they believe that, if they change their spouse for another one, everything will be all right and they can start a new life, wipe the slate clean and completely forget the past.

In reality that is not the case, although I am sure that is what is perceived by many at the time – that, following a new marriage, all former difficulties and troubles will disappear and pale into insignificance, the past will be forgotten and in a couple of years everyone will have recovered and everything in the garden will be absolutely lovely. Not so, I am afraid – and if this book achieves nothing else, I hope it will alert anyone thinking that way that they are being lied to by the father of lies, Satan. God has principles and laws in place, and they cannot be violated without harmful repercussions, just as with the law of gravity, whereby if you drop something, it goes down, not up. God has a pattern, and when we disobey His pattern for living, we pay the price one way or another.

Hurting people hurt people. Unhappy people tend to work at making others unhappy. The reason for this is sometimes deep rooted, and is not something that the person involved is aware of consciously. It can only be dealt with through repentance and prayer.

Sowing and reaping is a biblical law that should never be ignored, because it cannot fail. We reap what we sow. If we violate God's principles, things may go all right for a while, during a kind of honeymoon period, but there will definitely come a time when everything in the garden will be far from rosy.

God is our loving heavenly Father and wants so much to bless us with all good things, but every parent knows that when our children disobey and ignore our warnings, they take the consequences and sometimes as parents we just have to sit and wait for it to happen, as happen it will. Of course we still love them dearly and still want the best for them, and they are still our children, but they have been given a free will, like all of us, and they will take the consequences of what they do with that will.

Marriage is often entered into with one partner thinking that their spouse will change in time. The truth is that one person cannot change another person, which is what we all want to do when we run into difficulties – but it is possible for a person to allow themselves to be changed by choosing to let the Holy Spirit bring healing to those weak areas that constantly give them trouble. By allowing ourselves to be changed, we affect the environment in which we live, which in turn cannot fail to influence all those around us, whether we are aware of it or not.

A marriage partner, contrary to our reasoning, is totally unable to fill the void in our lives that most people become aware of at one time or another. Only God can do that. We often make the mistake of thinking that our husband or wife will fulfil us totally, when in fact that is an impossibility. It is only God, the One who designed and created us, who can fill that vast void which is within us all. When we allow God to envelop us completely and fill that ache within, and do not look to our marriage partner to do it, then our relationships are on a sure foundation. The Bible's good and sound advice is, 'In all your ways acknowledge Him and He shall direct your paths' (Proverbs 3:6 NKJV).

There is a lovely verse in the Old Testament which states that a cord of three strands is not easily broken (Ecclesiastes 4:12). In other words, by making a rope with three strands rather than just two, the strength is increased enormously. The same principle applies to a

Christian marriage. When both partners invite Jesus to help them in every aspect of their life together, then that relationship has a much greater chance of survival than if they were trying to struggle through on their own. It also takes a lot of pressure out of a marriage if you know that your spouse is looking to God to meet their needs when going through a personal crisis, instead of you. Nonetheless, although the verse says that the three-stranded cord is not easily broken, it does not say that it *cannot* be broken – but again, it is a matter of choice.

I do not wish to make myself look lily white and give the impression that I can do no wrong, because there are always faults on both sides when a relationship begins to run into trouble, even though it may have been initiated by one partner against the will of the other. Divorce is very rarely the answer to that trouble, however. In fact, it only adds to the problems, as we as a family have sadly found out.

Many years ago I also trespassed over the boundaries of our marriage by forming a very unhealthy relationship with another man. It was not intentional – I understand most of these things are not – and I certainly never desired to bring pain and hurt to my husband and family, whom I loved dearly. I knew I had ventured too far and had crossed a boundary, but I still carried on, until it was obvious that a potentially dangerous situation was rapidly arising. Eventually, as the relationship began to gather momentum, and after a lot of heart-searching and tears, we both walked away from the situation. By doing so, I believe we cut the ties that were beginning to bind us. It was most certainly not easy, and for some time afterwards my mind was in something of a turmoil. Then one day, a day that I can vividly recall, I was driving home after dropping my two eldest children at school when I felt a joy flood my whole body that I had never felt before – I can even remember where I was at the time it happened. I knew it was the joy of the Lord, and from that moment on I knew that God was assuring me that he had forgiven me and that I was free, and that the situation would never bother me again.

I am not proud of what I did, and that situation had the same potential to destroy my marriage as what was to happen to Bob years later. Yet, if I learned nothing else from the episode, I learned that the devil does go around like a roaring lion seeking whom he may devour. He hates Christian marriages, and if we are not continually on our guard, we run the risk of weaving a very tangled web. My marriage was happy, I had three small children, my husband was very good to me and we were very close, so I had no excuse. It is not always the marriages that are in trouble that end up on the rocks. People often say after an affair, 'We were happy – I don't know what came over me.'

The power of God's Word

When I was a child, my Sunday school superintendent and pastor encouraged me and the rest of the class to learn large passages of the Bible off by heart, and there was a prize each time we succeeded. I recall memorizing numerous psalms and large parts of Isaiah, as well as much of the New Testament. Those scriptures are still with me today. The version of the Bible that I memorized was the standard King James Version, which can now sometimes sound a little old fashioned with all its 'thee's and 'thou's, but I believe that those scriptures I learned as a child have had a tremendous impact on my life, in a way I could never have imagined at the time. The following verses prove that fact.

> Thy word have I hid in mine heart, that I might not sin against thee.
>
> PSALM 119:11

> Thy word is a lamp unto my feet, and a light unto my path.
>
> PSALM 119:105

> That from a child thou hast known the holy scriptures, which are able to make thee wise unto salvation through faith which is in Christ Jesus.
>
> 2 TIMOTHY 3:15

I believe the Word of God has had a great influence on me and has kept me throughout my life without me fully realizing it. Even though I now sometimes find it difficult to learn a scripture off by heart, I can still recite many of those passages that I learned as a young girl. Yet it is only recently that I have fully realized the power that the Word has to change lives and to renew our minds.

There is power in the Word, there is life in the Word, and it has absolute power to change us. God has given us His Word as a weapon of warfare and there are scriptures for every occasion that we face. In fact, John 1:1 tells us that God *is* the Word. It is not sufficient only to read it or even believe it; we need to walk in it, obey it, and let it change us into the people our Father desires us to be. He has a wonderful plan for me, as He has for you. We all have the same chance. The Bible is there for all of us to devour, and it will work for you as much as it will for me.

God knows how to use broken things in an ingenious way. He can take our broken lives and make them something beautiful. Once I gave the marriage breakdown to God, He started to bring about things in my life that I could hardly believe possible. In the first chapter of this book, I mentioned the building that God led us to in a miraculous way, and which is now being used by Release Foundation to train and disciple people, mainly those who feel the calling of God on their lives, to fully ground and instruct them in the Word of God in order that they may be released from previous negative influences and wrong thinking, that they may be able to realize their full potential in God. We marvel and thank Him every day for His amazing provision of this building. It was truly a gift from God.

A few months after we secured the building for our base, Release Foundation was offered a magnificent 90-foot yacht to be used in the work of God. It was offered to us by a Christian boat-builder in Zimbabwe, a master craftsman by the name of Tony Turner, who had felt that God had told him several years before to build the yacht to be used for His Kingdom. Zimbabwe, of course, is a land-locked country, so how did we manage to obtain a yacht from such a place? Only God can do things like this! Our first task was to find a skipper and crew willing to sail the yacht from Dar es Salaam, where it had been anchored for some time, up the coast of Africa, through the Red Sea and the Suez Canal, and into the Mediterranean Sea to northern Greece. Not being very familiar with the boating world, this posed us with one or two major problems, but once again God wonderfully undertook for us. Before we had even advertised, He supplied us with *two* Christian skippers and numerous crew members from all around the world, who also shared our vision of seeing lives changed in a powerful way as well as reaching out to the lost wide world.

Why did God choose us to be the ones to carry out this awesome vision? I do not know. In fact, taking charge of a yacht would certainly have been one of the very last things on my agenda. I am not a good sailor at the best of times. But God sure does work in very mysterious ways sometimes, and although some of His ways seem absolutely bizarre, if we learn to hear and obey His voice and put our trust in Him at all times and not dwell on the obstacles that face us, He will take us down paths – and waterways – that we could never have imagined in a thousand years!

The yacht, *Genevieve*, is now being used in the Mediterranean for various missions, both to reach people with the gospel message and to disciple and instruct Christians in their personal and spiritual growth, helping them to develop confidence in who they are in Christ. The aim is that everyone who sails in her will be mentored and built up in God as they relax and sail together, and that many truths from the Bible will be unfolded with the help of carefully chosen speakers and teachers.

I know that God still has a wonderful plan and purpose for my life, even though I now wear the dreaded label 'divorced', and I also know that if I let Him take control completely, many exciting things lie ahead, both in this life and in the next.

I am no different from anyone else – we all have the same Heavenly Father. Maybe even as you read this chapter, there is a part of your life that is still unresolved, or things that you have not been able to hand over to God. Do not hesitate any longer – do it now! Choose to let Him take complete control of your life. He knows how to set the captives free, and He knows just exactly what to do to help you in your particular need. No situation is ever so far gone that God cannot step in and completely change it. My God can do all things. Nothing is impossible with God – and I have wonderful news for you: He is your God too.

NINE

In everything, give thanks

You may have been wondering, as you have been reading my story, why I chose to write it. You have probably guessed that it was not an easy project, and it was one on which I had no need to embark.

So why would a woman like me want to share so many private thoughts and details of my life and experiences with the rest of the world? It would have been so much easier to have remained anonymous and simply got on with the rest of my life once Bob left.

Lessons to share

One of the reasons why I chose to share my story is because I believe that every difficulty and traumatic experience we go through in this life can build our character and bring us into the highest degree of God's blessing – *if* we allow ourselves to be set free and delivered from the situation in God's way. He has promised to deliver us from all our trials (Psalm 54:7). Having had to learn many hard lessons from my experiences, I wanted more than anything else to pass those lessons on to others, in the hope that at least some people might gain from my circumstances, without having to live through such trauma themselves.

Paul writes in 2 Corinthians 4:17, 'For our light affliction, which is but for a moment, is working for us an eternal weight of glory.' He goes on to say, in verse 18, 'For the things that are seen are temporary, but the things which are not seen are eternal' (NKJV). This scripture had a particular impact on me as I read it one day, even though I had read it dozens of times before. I felt that God was wanting to use this very difficult time in my life as a period of spiritual growth, and I began to realize that we learn most in times of difficulty, rather than in times of ease. Think about it. Fruit trees grow in the valleys, not on the mountain tops! Although as Christians we delight in 'mountain-top' experiences of joy in the presence of the Lord, it is actually when we are in a spiritual 'valley' that we are able to get closest to God, and the spiritual fruit within us begins to grow and ripen.

Although it is not a particularly popular thought, crisis is a part of life for everyone, young, old, rich, poor, single or married. Unfortunately, whether we like it or not, everyone experiences some kind of trauma in their life at one time or another. I am not talking about the everyday challenges and irritations that we all encounter, but about those unexpected tragedies and sudden storms that hit us and seek to shake us to the very core. Yet nobody really finds out who they are or what they are really made of until they have a time of real crisis and turmoil in their life. Ultimately, the most important thing is not what the crisis is, but that it is handled in such a way that we emerge victorious and totally free of those things that can keep us bound and restricted.

The tendency is to react to the difficulties and constantly dwell on the problems that we encounter, rather than taking positive action by fixing our eyes firmly on Jesus. He is able not only to deliver us from every trial, but also to completely heal and restore us, whatever situation or state we find ourselves in – even though our mind and flesh give us every indication that the opposite is true. When refining gold, a time of intense heat is required in order to bring impurities to the surface, but after a season in the midst of the fire, pure gold is produced.

The realization of this truth was one thing that carried me through some of my lowest points and darkest days. During my years as a Christian, I had experienced God's wonderful faithfulness to me, and I knew that He had promised He would never leave me and would be with me every step of the journey. Even through the pain,

I continually sensed the Lord's presence. I also sensed that I was growing a little stronger each day as I learned to put my faith in Him, even though every single prop seemed to have been removed from my life.

Remember that 2 Corinthians 4:18 declares that the things we cannot see are eternal. We need to hold on to that fact when the intensity of the situation and the state of our mind threatens to destroy us. The truth is that all the while, God is working behind the scenes and building us into the people He desires us to be. We need to put our full trust in Him, even when all around us is looking pretty grim and we cannot see the wood for the trees!

So what about the person who feels that the only way forward is for them to leave their spouse? Even common sense would decree that it is best to think through carefully the long- and short-term implications of such an action. It might be wise not to close any doors that cannot be reopened. It might also be wise not to enter into another relationship to try to deaden the hurt, as it will only lead to further complications.

God always blesses faithfulness and commitment, and if the decision to stay together at this difficult time is honoured, the rewards could very well be immense. God has given us all emotions, and breaking up a relationship is a highly emotional situation when it is almost impossible for those involved to think straight. I guarantee that six months down the line you will be glad you did not rush headlong into something which your heart was saying you must do immediately.

I am fully aware that there are some situations that are very complex and that initially the best solution all round would seem to be for the couple to part, at least for a period of time. I also know, however, that there is not a single complicated relationship that God is not able to turn around for His glory and our good. I firmly believe that there is not a single marriage that God cannot revive and resurrect. He is God, and His ways are different from our ways. His thinking and timing are so different, too. Nothing, not even that difficult relationship, is too hard for Him to change.

Nevertheless, I also happen to believe that there are times when divorce would seem sadly inevitable. Even though some would disagree with me, I would never advise anyone to stay in an abusive or violent marriage, or if the couple are each determined to go their separate ways no matter what. Having said that, I do know that the living God is even able to bring such couples to reconciliation, if each partner is willing to let Him have complete control, and if they both allow Him to take the reins of their lives, bringing peace and total fulfilment into an otherwise hopeless situation.

Apart from wishing to share with others the lessons I learned, I also had another reason for writing this book. I wanted to reach those of you who have, like me, gone through a painful divorce or broken relationship, in the hope of reassuring you that it is possible to be released from the anguish and trauma that marital breakdown brings, however bad it has been, and it is possible to learn to repent of any hurts either wilfully or inadvertently caused. With God's help, it is also possible to overlook all the wrongs that have been done to you, and to forgive by obeying the Word of God and walking in His ways. It need not take a lifetime if we trust God! In our own strength it is impossible, because we are all weak and constantly struggle with our mind and emotions. Yet when we put our hand in the hand of the Lord, just like a little toddler might hold the hand of a parent, He will lead the way.

Once again, it is a matter of choice. We have to choose to let God minister healing and restoration to us in His own powerful way. He will not force us against our will or make us conform to His ways, as each of us has freedom of choice. Of course, liberation and release from the shame and hurts of the past do not just happen in a moment – it is sometimes a very painful process that has to be carefully and patiently worked through, with the help and guidance of our Heavenly Father.

During difficult times of emotional turmoil, God might be the last thought on our mind, but it is a fact that once we call on God and completely cast our care upon Him, all those things that the devil meant for bad and to bring harm and destruction into our lives, God can turn around for our good in a way that our best friend or counsellor could never do. After all, I am sure the One who made us knows how best to guide us through troubled times, no matter how far we feel we might have strayed from Him.

One of the most ancient stories in the Bible is that of Job. He was a God-fearing man who experienced disaster after disaster. In a very short period of time he lost all his children – seven sons and three daughters – as well as his livelihood and his health. Then his 'friends' came round to give him some 'good advice'. Even today they are often referred to as 'Job's comforters'. They had totally misread the whole process through which Job was going, and their advice was therefore from their own understanding and did not come out of their faith and trust in God.

Most of us have people and friends who rally round us in times of trouble. Some of them speak words of wisdom to us and some do not. Some people, even those closest to us, can talk us out of the truth and persuade us to pursue a wrong path, perhaps because they have challenges in their own life or marriage and if we fail, it makes them feel better about their own past indiscretions and mistakes. It acts as a kind of justification for them.

In spite of everything Job's so-called friends said, which brought doom and gloom into his life, the Bible records that at the end of the story Job started to pray for these folk who had unwittingly tried to get him to do and say things which would have led him into even more trouble. The Bible also tells us that when Job began to pray for his friends, God started to bless him again in an abundant manner. Indeed, God blessed him so much that Job finished up with double the amount of everything he had started out with – and at the beginning of the story we are told he was a very wealthy man.

There are many interpretations one can put on that story. One of them certainly is that when we start to take our eyes off our own immediate problems and begin to reach out to meet the needs of others, even though our heart may be breaking at the time, God then reaches out to us and begins to deal with our own difficulties, which gradually pale into insignificance. It is almost as though we need to take our hands off our own trying situation before the Lord is truly able to take charge and change the circumstances in our life, in a way that we could never have envisaged.

A matter of choice

One of the difficulties we have in the Western world, which applies to both Christians and non-Christians alike, is that we have the wrong notion of what love really is. Contrary to common belief, and contrary to what our instincts frequently tell us, love is not a feeling. Yes, you read it right. Love is not a feeling. Obviously our flesh and our emotions are involved when we fall in love with someone, but I still say that love is not a feeling; it is a decision – a choice. You choose to love someone.

The phrase 'love your neighbour' is quoted over half a dozen times in the Bible, but if love was a feeling we could argue and say, 'Well, I don't feel that I love them.' Yet love is a decision that we make – a very important one, but one that is often taken very lightly indeed. It is not only a decision that we make for ourselves, however: we are *commanded* to love (John 13:34).

The same principle applies with a husband and wife, or with any human relationship for that matter. If we start to do loving things to those around us, they will automatically respond – bearing in mind once again the biblical principle 'give and it will be given to you'. It works – because it is the Word of God and it is His pattern for living. It has absolutely no option but to work.

If love is not a choice, why does God tell us to love our enemies? He does not say that we have to like them or agree with them – but we are to love them. Why? Because love never fails. That is the ultimate. Although our mind, feelings and instincts may be telling us the opposite, we must remember that God's way is perfect and when we apply love to a situation, the situation changes. Love is a choice. It is an act of the will, if you like. You choose to love someone. We can also choose to love God in the same way. That is another command, in fact, because to love the Lord our God with all our heart, mind and strength is the basis of our faith. 'Jesus replied, "Love the Lord your God with all your heart and with all your soul and with all your mind." This is the first and greatest commandment. And the second is like it: "Love your neighbour as yourself." All the Law and the Prophets hang on these two commandments' (Matthew 22:37-40).

I am not saying that to love is easy. In fact, it is something with which many of us constantly struggle. Yet so many things in life are to do with choice, with making right decisions – decisions that come into line with God and His Word and not with our own understanding. After all, most things in life which are worth having do not come easily. You have to work hard to achieve them and make many sacrifices, but the outcome is well worth the effort.

The book of Galatians talks about the fruit of the Spirit, attributes we can receive once we have the Holy Spirit dwelling within us. The attributes mentioned in Galatians 5:22 are love, joy, peace, long-suffering, kindness, goodness, faithfulness, gentleness and self-control. In Matthew 12:33, Jesus makes this obvious but important statement: make a tree good and its fruit will be good, but make a tree bad and its fruit will be bad, for a tree is recognized by its fruit.

We cannot achieve these attributes in our own strength. How many of us have proudly announced that we have made New Year's resolutions, only to fail miserably and break them a week later? In ourselves we are weak, and we can only bear much fruit as we allow God to bring about a gradual change in our life. Again it is a matter of choice. We have to choose to obey God and allow Him to deal with us in certain areas, and gradually the fruit will be evident in every part of our lives, especially as we learn to abide in Him. It is a gradual process, however, which takes time and much discipline on our part.

I believe that to have the fruit of the Spirit is more important than to exercise a special gift that God in His love might have given us. What is the good of being gifted and having talents, if we do not have the right attitude and character to exercise those talents, and are critical and self-seeking, with no fruit of the Spirit evident in our lives? We will do more damage than good to the Kingdom of God.

We have to choose to love rather than hate, to be joyful rather than sorrowful, to be at peace rather than full

of strife, to be patient rather than impatient, and to forgive when we really do not feel like it. It is not easy.
Indeed, it appears to be in complete opposition to what
our mind and our flesh tell us is right, and it is something
that has to be constantly worked at. The choice is ours.

It is not easy to act in a way opposite to how we are
feeling, but that is what God requires of us at times, if we
are to be obedient to the precepts of the Bible and if we
are to find total fulfilment in life. When God's precepts
are obeyed, the benefits and rewards are absolutely end-
less. If we keep doing what we know is right, ultimately
the feelings will follow. The right actions will come to
seem natural as the Holy Spirit is allowed to do His work
in us and through us.

I have heard people say that they could not perform
actions which go against the way they feel because that
would be hypocritical. This is an argument that the devil
uses to stop us from obeying God's commands. In short,
if our feelings do not line up with biblical principles,
we have to do something about it if we are to be overcomers and live a joyful and victorious life.

The way we have done things all our life is not nec-
essarily God's way. That can only be achieved with the
help of the Holy Spirit as He reveals issues in our life
that need changing and resolving. We must therefore
learn to let the truth of God's Word penetrate our very
being, thus renewing our mind. If we want to lead happy
and fruitful lives and honour God in everything we do,
we have to get to the root cause of any problems that we
encounter. It is no good – as I discovered to my cost –

taking the easy way out and ignoring matters that need to be faced, pushing difficulties under the carpet, or trying to avoid painful issues that really ought to be brought out into the open. That is simply like pulling off the tops of weeds and leaving the roots behind. Eventually the weeds will spring up once more and then the whole process has to be lived through once again.

Handing things over to God

Another thing that God has taught me over the last few years is to release things – and people – to Him, and trust Him completely for a happy and fruitful outcome. There are people who can hurt us deeply in life, but they have to be handed over to God without us endeavouring to get our own back. If we do that, we are taking matters into our own hands instead of leaving God to bring justice to the situation. Proverbs 20:22 says the following: 'Do not say, "I'll pay you back for this wrong!" Wait for the LORD, and he will deliver you' (NIV).

The Bible talks a great deal about how to deal with our enemies. We are to love our enemies and pray for those who persecute us. That is contrary to our natural way of thinking and feeling. The Bible also says, 'If your enemy is hungry, feed him; if he is thirsty, give him a drink' (Romans 12:20 NKJV). Probably the last thing we would think to do naturally would be to feed our enemy if he turned up hungry on our doorstep – but when we obey God and do it, regardless of our instincts, not only will we feel a whole lot better, but we will definitely change. More to the point, so will our enemy!

Having an unforgiving attitude towards those who have wronged us can without doubt produce harmful and long-term consequences in our life. It opens the door to bitterness and hurt, twin enemies that will wreak spiritual and emotional havoc, leaving us impoverished and weakened. That is a far cry from the freedom and security God wants us to enjoy. It was therefore a very practical instruction that Jesus gave His followers to forgive their enemies, and He was a perfect example of this. On the cross He asked His Father to forgive those involved in His painful death.

I recently came across a dictionary of proverbs and sayings from around the world. As I flipped casually through its pages, one suddenly caught my attention: 'It is good to make a bridge of gold to a flying enemy.' Intrigued, I looked up the definition, and this is what it said: 'When an enemy is defeated, it is wise to let him make good his escape, lest he turn to fight again because his route has been cut off.'

As I thought about this, I began to realize the wisdom of making a way of escape for those things in our life – such as unforgiveness – which, like flesh-and-blood enemies, will constantly come back to bother us if we do not let them go. This was a new thought to me. I knew, of course, about the concept of building bridges to close a gap in a relationship – but to build a bridge in order to allow something as ugly and harmful as unforgiveness to escape was a new and exciting idea. I totally believe that each bridge we take the trouble to build can bring pure gold into our lives, allowing us to be free of our 'enemies' for evermore.

Living in freedom

Freedom is a word that is often discussed in today's society. Understandably, everyone wants to be free from the things that dominate and control them. Christians often talk about freedom and like to listen to sermons preached about walking free and becoming liberated. The sad thing is that many of us never grasp the real truths that are able to bring freedom into our lives in the way the Lord is longing to see happen.

Many folk also mistakenly think that to be free means that they can do what they like. This is far from the real truth. In order to experience the freedom the Bible talks about, not only do we have to meditate and feed on the Word, but we also need to obey it, allowing the Word to bring about a complete transformation in our life. I believe it is impossible to obey God and not be wonderfully and mightily blessed. This is very much the sentiment of Matthew 6:33: 'Seek ye first the kingdom of God, and his righteousness; and all these things shall be added unto you' (KJV).

What are 'these things'? I believe they are the things Jesus died that we might have. They are ours for the taking when we are obedient to God. If we do that, not only will we have our everyday needs met, but our relationships – even those challenging ones – will thrive and flourish. We will then be able to come into all the fullness of life that God has promised us. If you want to be free, you cannot run from every trial and hardship that comes your way. Freedom means no longer being bound by shame, bitterness and past hurts. It means being able to forgive and overlook offences. Being free inside is more important than being able to do as we please. John 8:36 tells us, 'If the Son sets you free, you will be free indeed' (NIV).

When you are on your way to experiencing complete freedom, you know it! The happiest animals are those that are trained and know their boundaries. They know what their master expects of them. The problem is that very often the way God indicates for us to go is exactly the opposite to the way our mind and emotions urge us to proceed. A verse in Proverbs gives us the advice that we need to hear: 'Trust in the LORD with all your heart and lean not on your own understanding' (Proverbs 3:5). Even if it is a difficult struggle at first, if we follow after God's truth we will be rewarded, as we are reminded in John 8:32: 'Then you will know the truth, and the truth will set you free' (NIV).

The book of Isaiah also talks about freedom, and God's views on the subject. 'The Spirit of the Sovereign LORD is on me, because the LORD has anointed me to preach good news to the poor. He has sent me to bind up the broken-hearted, to proclaim freedom for the captives and release from darkness for the prisoners' (Isaiah 61:1). God is just longing to open the prison gates and to set prisoners free! He is longing to replace our mourning with joy and gladness. Some people can be imprisoned by circumstances for most of their lives, sometimes of their own making, at other times through no fault of their own – until they suddenly realize that the prison doors are open and there is a way of escape.

It is very interesting to note how many key people in the Bible were in prison at one point or another in their lives. Paul and Silas, for instance, were thrown into jail for evangelizing and talking about Jesus, and although they had been undeservedly beaten and chained up, at around midnight they began to sing praises to God – not the thing that most people would be expected to do in that situation. Yet, as they did, the chains that held them captive were broken, the prison doors flew open, and they gained their freedom (Acts 16:25). They totally ignored the fact that they had been so very wrongly and unjustly treated, and praised God regardless.

Like any journey, we have to take the first step ourselves – which is to get in line with what the Bible says, even though it may seem totally opposed to how we are feeling. It will be a struggle, but if we take that first step, the Lord will meet us in a powerful way and the situation in which we find ourselves will miraculously change, because we are now doing things according to His instructions. All I can say to you is this: it works.

I guess we have all bought something that needs to be put together before we can use it, and in our eagerness to start we ignore the directions on how to assemble it until we find that we are running into difficulties. Then we are forced to do what we should have done in the first place, which is to consult the maker's instructions. Life is often very similar. Many of the problems we encounter could be avoided if only we would decide to live our life according to God's guidebook, the Bible. To those who take the time to read them, the instructions are clear. We sometimes think that we know best, but the real truth is that our Heavenly Father is the one who knows best. He knows us far better than we know ourselves, and He knows exactly those things we need.

Paul and Silas had every right to grumble and complain. As they were going about spreading the good news of the gospel, they were captured and thrown into jail. How dreadfully unfair – but they still chose to make that sacrifice of praise. They praised God when the chips were down, and God faithfully met them and delivered them from the chains that bound them.

The Bible states quite clearly that the devil comes to rob, steal and destroy. That is his main aim and purpose, and it is true that he has robbed and stolen from many, but we are also warned that we should not be ignorant of the devil's devices. The Bible sums up the whole situation well when it states in Hosea 4:6, 'My people are destroyed from lack of knowledge' (NIV). We can be people of God, loving Him and wanting to serve Him, but at the same time we can also be ignorant and lack knowledge of the truth, which means that the devil can use that ignorance to deceive and cheat us, robbing us of what God wants us to have as His dearly loved children. The enemy loves to keep us ignorant of the truth because, sadly, more so than some Christians, he knows that the truth is able to set all who find it gloriously free.

We should keep in our minds the fact that the devil is up to no good. He likes nothing better than to see us turn away from God. Satan loves it when the Word of God fails to find a resting place within us, and even causes us to misinterpret Scripture so that we are kept from the truth and from the freedom Jesus died to give us. The word 'free' is not in the devil's vocabulary. He wants us to remain bound in the shame of our past mistakes and experiences, but Jesus died that we might have life and have it more abundantly. If Satan cannot snuff out our faith, he will certainly try to divert us away from the purposes of God and get us on a different road, maybe even the road to ruin. I can guarantee that it will not be the road that can lead us to freedom.

Choosing to follow God

We often take the line of least resistance, whatever seems easiest to us, but each time we do that, we will probably very soon find ourselves in the same situation again, faced with the same difficult choices. Someone once said, 'Decisions are a serious business. We can have all that God has for us, or we can spend the rest of our lives wondering what things we might have missed by our disobedience.' What we are today is a result of yesterday's choices.

God allowed many people we read about in the Bible to go through very difficult experiences. Joshua brought down the walls of Jericho, but only after he had very carefully obeyed the instructions given to him by God. Shadrach, Meshach and Abednego were thrown into a fiery furnace because they would not bow down and worship a false God, and the king commanded that the furnace be made seven times hotter than usual before they were thrown in. Not only did they miraculously survive the ordeal, but when they emerged it is recorded that not even their clothes had the smell of smoke upon them, and they themselves were totally unharmed. The only things that had been destroyed were the ropes that had bound them. Probably the greatest story of deliverance, however, is that of the Children of Israel who walked through the Red Sea to dry land as the Egyptian army pursued them. When the Egyptians tried to follow them across, horses and riders alike were drowned.

The point that links all these stories is that the people involved obeyed the leading and prompting of God, and consequently only had to go through those particular trials once. In Numbers 33:3 we read about the Children of Israel who came out of Egypt with a 'high hand' because they obeyed God, who told them that they would never have to go through that particular situation again. God is a God of deliverance. He is able to rescue us from every tribulation if we trust Him and acknowledge Him in everything we do.

We often hear of history repeating itself, and of people going through the same situation over and over again. Very often this is because they did not go through the situation God's way and according to the pattern that

He ordained. The reason for this is probably that they did not fully comprehend what was really happening. They did not understand that there were strongholds in their life that needed to be severely dealt with and broken once and for all.

God has a glorious plan for each of our lives, but it might take a very long time to get there if we insist on doing things our way. Even though we may be in the middle of a situation that we know should never really have happened – and we can question it until the day we die – it is possible to know that, in spite of our lack of understanding and our disobedience, God still has a plan and a purpose for our life. He can turn our mess into a miracle and replace all the bad things with good, if we allow Him to steer us through it and do not take matters into our own hands.

I believe with all my heart that with God it is possible to come through absolutely anything, and that the most dire situation, given to God, need not end in ruin. I want as many people as possible to see that the biblical ways and principles that God has set out are as immovable as the laws of nature, because the Living God Himself has set them in place.

We need to remember this fact: what we sow, we reap. That is a very important biblical law, often quoted even by those who do not believe the Bible. Logic tells us that we reap from the seeds we sow. If we sow to the flesh, we reap to the flesh, but if we sow to the Spirit, we reap to the Spirit. If we plant onions, we get onions in return, not roses. You do not need a degree to work that one out.

There is no timescale attached to reaping what we sow. God has not synchronized His watch to ours, because He does not have the same kind of timescale as us. He does not live in time at all. In our instant, 'get it now' society, we no sooner think about something than we want it. Yet whatever God has for us, He will give us when He sees we are ready – in His time. That could be 20 years away, or it could be tomorrow – but it will still be in God's time. We must be content with the fact that God is never early, nor is He ever late.

My heart's desire is that through this book many will choose to dump their hang-ups and begin to live on a higher level by coming into a greater understanding of the truth of the Word of God. It has absolute power and authority to change lives – your life, my life, the life of anyone who is willing to take their hands off the steering wheel and allow God to guide them through even the most difficult moments of their lives, regardless of how complicated and desperate their past has been.

Some situations with which we are faced in life completely knock us off our feet. Initially I am sure most of us react in the same way and go through all the normal emotions, but as long as we do not *stay* emotionally sick, but choose to press on, we are on our way to being what the Bible calls 'an overcomer'. I believe one of the keys to rising above any situation is to come to the understanding that it is ourselves we have to deal with and not the other person, even if they seem to be the cause of all our trouble and despair.

Even if someone has wronged us badly, and has told lies about us or mistreated us in a way we simply do not deserve, it is absolutely no use trying to change them or refusing to talk to them until they apologize. Our own attitude and condition of heart are the most important issues with which we should be dealing. How we handle the situation is of the uttermost importance and will almost certainly pave the way for our future wellbeing and freedom.

We may spend a lifetime hating someone or harbouring an offence for something someone has done to us, feeling that we are possibly punishing them in some way. If we do that, however, we will without a shadow of a doubt be the out-and-out loser, and not them – in fact, they may not even know that we are angry, or they may not even realize that they have hurt us. They appear to get off free, and we are the one in bondage, carrying their transgressions.

I am sure that is one of the reasons why Jesus asks us to love our enemies – not because He wants our enemies to get away with murder, so to speak, but because He wants us to be free and to live abundantly according to His promises, trusting Him to take care of our so-called enemies. God is God, and He is divinely qualified to take care of those people in our life who have wronged us.

I would love to be able to tell you that I have never wronged anybody in my life, but that would simply not be the truth. We all hurt people, especially those close to us, at some time or another, whether intentionally or not, and I am sure we would like to think that forgiveness would be extended to us at such times. If we refuse to forgive, the Bible tells us that we will not ourselves be forgiven. Jesus has forgiven us all so much, even the sins that we are yet to commit. As children of God, we have no option but to forgive each other if we are to lead contented, happy and fulfilled lives. We are told that we must 'do to others what you would have them do to you' (Matthew 7:12).

Bitterness and hatred will not only take their toll on our health, but will also hinder us from becoming all that God has purposed us to be. After all, God is much more able to bring justice into a situation than we are. I believe that when we try to get our own back on someone, God folds His arms and says, 'OK, carry on and do it your way, but you'll make a mess!' He is a God of love, and love sometimes means discipline and correction. We in turn should learn to relax and cast our cares upon the Lord and let Him fight our battles, leaving us free to carry on with our lives in a happy and peaceful manner, praising God regardless. This is what 1 Thessalonians 5:16 says: 'Be joyful always; pray continually; give thanks in all circumstances, for this is God's will for you in Christ Jesus.'

Divorce is a very nasty word as far as I am concerned, and it is a subject I would never have imagined myself writing about. A few short years ago, the very thought would have seemed impossible. Nonetheless, although I now find myself on a totally different path in life, and I sometimes feel completely out of my comfort zone, I believe with all my heart that if I allow God to bring divine health and healing to those areas that threaten ruin and destruction,

He will guide my steps. I know that while I am on this planet, God has a purpose and destiny for me, and it is one that only God Himself can help me realize.

It is, of course, possible in situations like this to give the appearance of recovery while ignoring the true root cause of the problem. If we do not let God, through His Word, deal with some of the painful issues in our life that need attention, we could end up with many regrets, and perhaps also with hurts and abuses from the past still unresolved. I am fairly sure that, if you have ever travelled abroad on an airline with a bulging suitcase, you will know that excess baggage has a very high price tag attached to it. Far better to be like the eagle mentioned in Isaiah, able to soar and glide in the warm thermals, free from all the earthbound restrictions that less fortunate creatures know. This is the promise waiting for all those who do things God's way. 'Those who hope in the LORD will renew their strength. They will soar on wings like eagles; they will run and not grow weary, they will walk and not be faint' (Isaiah 40:31).

TEN

Friends — special gifts from God

As I write this book, it is still less than three years since Bob finally left the family home and filed for divorce, which became absolute 12 months later. Looking back, I am amazed at the processes through which God has taken me during that comparatively short period of time, and at all that I have been able to learn as a result. Not only did He deal with many painful issues in my life and challenge many areas of weakness within me, but I was also aware that the Lord was leading and guiding me through each situation, and I believed that as long as I kept close to

Him, He would carry me and I would be protected from all that could potentially engulf me.

There is, of course, a natural healing process that follows any trauma we experience, but I believe the most important thing is not what we have gone through, but how we handle those difficult situations – and Jesus has shown us that loving and forgiving people is definitely the best and most rewarding way to deal with circumstances that might otherwise destroy us. Recovery times will vary from situation to situation, because as individuals we each respond differently to the circumstances we experience.

Friendships form a vitally important part of most people's lives, and in times of great turmoil and change it is often the case that new friends are made and other friendships sometimes sadly fade. Who we choose as our friends and companions can make a very big impact on our lives. In a previous chapter I commented on the so-called friends of Job, but there are also other, more positive examples of friendship in the Bible. The relationship between David and Jonathan (1 Samuel 18 onwards) is a lovely example of what a good friendship can be like when it is formed on a solid foundation and is rooted in God. Jesus, at the end of His ministry, told His disciples that He no longer called them servants but friends, because He had intimately shared with them everything that His Father had told Him (John 15:15).

I believe that God in His mercy brings many different people into our lives during troubled times, to enrich, encourage and even challenge us, just when we need them most. It is when we feel alone in the world and everything seems against us that God steps in, fulfilling His promise that He will never leave us or forsake us (Deuteronomy 31:6). I am also often reminded of the scripture which says, 'If God is for us, who can be against us?' (Romans 8:31)

It is vitally important that the people whom we choose to walk beside us in life as close friends have a positive rather than negative effect on us. When people run into marital difficulties or go through divorce, there is a definite tendency for them to forsake their long-term friends whose own relationships have stood the test of time, and instead be drawn to circles of people who have been through similar experiences, or who would never disagree with them or challenge what they are doing.

Home alone

After Bob left, I had no option but to live entirely alone for the next six months in the family home, our two daughters having married and flown the nest just a few months before. I had never suffered from loneliness in the past. In fact, when the children were still living with us I looked forward to the rare occasions when I had the house to myself for a short while. Nonetheless, when isolation was thrust upon me suddenly and unexpectedly, with the distinct prospect of permanency, it was a totally different thing. Our home had always seemed to be bursting with life while we were bringing up our family, and a kind of panic set in as I realized that living totally alone for the long-term future could be the shape of things to come for me.

As I look back now on those six months, however, I consider them to be a very valuable period of my life. I was able to spend time praying and crying out to God in my distress – and God met me in a most powerful way as He began to work in my life, highlighting areas that needed dealing with. It was a very painful process, but at the same time I knew that God had heard my prayers and was meeting me in a way that I would never previously have dared to believe was possible.

He also sent good solid people into my life who not only nurtured and cared for me, but also challenged me as they lovingly undertook some straight talking which greatly enriched my walk with the Lord. We all need dependable people around us who can hear from God when we are unable, in our distressed state, to think clearly ourselves. We all need friends who have the courage to challenge different areas of our lives, even though our first reaction might be to run from them. I believe that these special people are sent by God Himself and are the channels which He uses to speak gently to us. Although sometimes we look upon such people as being 'against us', they are probably the very people we need at that particular time.

One thing I was determined not to do was to hold 'pity parties' or join clubs with other women who had recently been divorced, or were in the process of being divorced. I felt that, if I was to make a complete recovery, I had to avoid that type of situation – but obviously, if getting together with someone in a similar situation would have had a positive input into *their* life, such as being able to share scriptural principles with them, then that would have been a valid thing to do.

God is our source

Thankfully, the church to which I belong is also very caring, and reaches out to people with diverse problems and needs. True to form, I found that many of the folk at the Fellowship, including those in authority, rallied round and made time to visit, pray for and write to me. Sometimes people with whom I had only exchanged a few words would call at just the right moment, bringing words of hope. Without the care and loving concern of these good people, I am sure my recovery would have been so much slower. They were living out the instruction that Paul gave to the church in Rome: 'Rejoice with them that do rejoice, and weep with them that weep' (Romans 12:15 KJV).

As Christians I believe we are all called to care for each other, because we are all part of God's family. When people are hurting very badly, however, we often try to avoid them because we feel so helpless and lost for words. We do not know what to say or do, so we hang back and do nothing. I am sure, however, that every little bit of love and care we give to each other, even though it may seem very small and futile at the time, is used by God in His own unique way.

When I first began to realize that my marriage might be breaking up, my immediate thought was to go far away from everyone to whom I normally related, in order to try to distance myself from the guilt, shame, hurt and rejection that I was feeling. I just wanted to disappear. I wanted to be somewhere where no one could find me. I felt second rate and a complete failure. I was obviously reacting to the dire circumstances in which I suddenly found myself, instead of responding in a positive way and putting my whole trust in God – but this was a reaction that I now realize was completely understandable and certainly not uncommon.

In addition, because of the complexity of our particular situation, everyone else to whom I would normally have looked for help – my pastor, my church friends, my family and even those who worked for us – was also trying to come to terms with what was happening. They were all personally involved in one way or another, and it was not easy for me to talk to them while they were struggling to deal with their own hurts and damaged emotions.

I remember toying with the idea of catching the next plane to Zimbabwe in order to be with my good friends Rob and Hilary Mackenzie. I felt that I needed to be in a different environment, but at the same time I wanted people to talk to with whom I felt comfortable: I felt these two factors would allow me to think more clearly. Fortunately, I saw sense and came to the conclusion that it would not in fact be the best of times to disappear off the scene. I eventually decided that I really ought to be at home, facing the situation head on, as well as being around for my children should they need me. I also thought that, if there was to be any hope of reconciliation between Bob and myself, putting so much distance between us and the children at that point would not be a particularly good idea.

On the very same evening that I decided to stay around and not run and hide, I walked into my study to find a fax waiting for me from Rob and Hilary. They knew absolutely nothing yet of the situation I was facing, but I discovered to my amazement that they were arriving in England the next morning. They were making the journey because their two-year-old son Mark needed urgent medical treatment in London. It was not the best of reasons for them to be coming back to Britain, but I immediately gave thanks to God as I knew that He had supplied my need at exactly the right moment. He knows just what we need and who to put around us at any given time. He is also able to move people all over the globe just as He pleases. Distance is no object to Him!

Although Rob and Hilary originally thought that they would be in Britain for not much more than a few weeks, complications with Mark's condition stretched their stay to six months. The time allowed Mark to recover fully, but also gave us much more time together than we had initially thought likely. They were a tremendous source of blessing to me at a very difficult and crucial time of my life, in spite of the fact that they themselves were walking a very painful path with their young son's illness. The Mackenzies had been good friends of both Bob and myself long before our troubles started, so our accelerating situation only added more sadness to the medical problems they were facing with Mark. As it turned out, I think we were all able to be a source of comfort to each other as we talked and prayed together during those very difficult months.

Often in the first few months after Bob had left, when I was feeling very low and despair was beginning to set in, someone would turn up unexpectedly on my doorstep to pray for me, bring flowers or give me a word of encouragement – or the phone would ring just when I needed to talk to someone. On several occasions I was just throwing the last of the dead flowers in the dustbin when the doorbell rang – and there was a florist delivering yet another bouquet! I could, of course, have got by without a steady supply of flowers, but to me they underlined the love and care that God had for me. Through a gift that He had personally designed and created, He showed me that He loved me deeply, and that He was wanting to minister to my emotional needs as well as every other area of my life, reinforcing my strong belief that He did know and care, and that He would always be there beside me whatever happened.

One lady who was a real pillar of strength to me at that time was my neighbour, Sandra Bonner. She and her husband Mick, who pastors a church in Coventry, had lived in the house opposite us for years. In spite of their close proximity and the fact that we are all born-again Christians, we could go months without seeing each other – largely due, I guess, to our busy lifestyles. So I was quite surprised one morning when Sandra appeared at my door, smiling warmly but looking a little pensive. 'Pat, I don't quite know how to put this,' she started, once I had invited her into the kitchen for a coffee, 'but over the last few days I keep feeling that I need to pray for you, and even though I do, the burden won't go away. I was just wondering if there was anything specific that you needed prayer for right now?'

I know for a fact that Sandra had absolutely no idea what had been going on in my life, but in spite of that, she was sufficiently in tune with the Lord to know that I needed prayer! I admired her courage and obedience in coming over to see me, having heard from God clearly what she should do. It would have been so much easier for her to have ignored what she was feeling, rather than risk looking foolish if she had heard incorrectly. Following that first visit, she came over regularly to talk and pray, with never a single negative word coming out of her mouth. What is more, I knew that Sandra and her family were close by and willing to help, should I need them. We still meet regularly, and I greatly value her friendship and the wise counsel that she gives.

Christians belong to a worldwide family, and I discovered that people as far away as Australia, South Africa and the USA were praying for me on a regular basis. This was a very comforting thing to know, as well as very humbling. Words can never adequately express just how grateful I am for everyone who supported me at that time. Without taking away a thing from what they did, however, I know that the times I was able to spend alone with the Lord were the most precious, as He revived and renewed my passion for Him.

I also know that God rewards everyone who faithfully sacrifices their time in order to minister healing to the hurting and help bind up the broken-hearted, and I rest content in the fact that those people who are dear to my heart will one day reap the reward for the deeds they have done. Good friends are truly a gift from God, but we must never forget that it is God alone who is our source. As the Bible states, 'In Your presence is fullness of joy; At Your right hand are pleasures forevermore' (Psalm 16:11 NKJV).

Renewing our minds

Learning to listen to the voice of the Holy Spirit is vital in our walk with Him. Yet listening to His voice is only half the exercise: it is important also to learn to trust and obey His leading. In times of trouble there are often a number of routes we could take, and it is possible to feel torn in all directions, especially if our mind is in turmoil. The devil can play tricks with our mind and our thoughts, convincing us that right is wrong and wrong is right. It is easy, when you are in an emotionally distressed state, to be completely thrown off track.

God does not just want to change our hearts; He wants to change our minds too, so that we learn to think the way He thinks. Once this process has commenced, we are not so likely to be pushed around by the dangerous urgings of our flesh and emotions. Paul, writing to the church in Rome, says that believers need to have their minds renewed, a concept that can sometimes be overlooked by modern-day Christians. 'Do not conform any longer to the pattern of this world, but be transformed by the renewing of your mind. Then you will be able to test and approve what God's will is – his good, pleasing and perfect will' (Romans 12:2).

People – not only those in the secular world, but also sadly some Christians – often admit that they have an empty void inside that they are unable to explain or fill. Those of us who have entrusted our lives to God know that the emptiness can only be filled by doing just that: by allowing God to come into our lives and take complete control. 'Blessed are those who hunger and thirst for righteousness, for they will be filled' (Matthew 5:6).

I believe that we are living in tremendously exciting times, when God is doing great things and people all over the globe are finding the Lord in a miraculous way. Some who have been believers for years are being released in a moment from things that have bound them for a long time. Their deep longing is being replaced with a peace that goes far beyond all human comprehension, and with a hope that only God Himself can give. It is certainly a great time to be alive! 'And the peace of God, which passeth all understanding, shall keep your hearts and minds through Christ Jesus' (Philippians 4:7 KJV).

All over the world, Christians are also rediscovering the power and authority of the Word of God, as well as their own spiritual authority as they allow themselves to be guided by the Holy Spirit and gain fresh insight into all that God has for them as His children. The Bible makes it plain that salvation cannot be earned, but is a gift, and therefore we do not have to attain some super-spiritual plateau before God can use us. If that were the case, we would never be used by God! Jesus' death on the cross and His resurrection have dealt with the question of our sin once and for all.

Meditation – a life-changing exercise

I have found it to be a liberating and life-changing exercise to meditate on the Word of God. As I concentrated and thought through passages of Scripture, including some that I had known since childhood, I discovered that they took on a new relevance as I uncovered gems of truth that had always been there, but needed a little spadework to be revealed. I began to see many passages in the Bible from a different perspective as I gave thought to them while driving to appointments, lying in bed at night, washing up or just staring into space. I discovered that meditation leads to revelation, and revelation which is acted upon changes people for ever. It produces 'fruit that lasts', changes that become evident in our lives. Fruit is a food, and if we bear good fruit, we are able to feed a hungry and very needy world. 'Do not let this Book of the Law depart from your mouth; meditate on it day and night, so that you may be careful to do everything written in it. Then you will be prosperous and successful' (Joshua 1:8). What a wonderful verse!

One of God's promises is that in the last days He will pour out His Holy Spirit on all flesh (Joel 2:20) – and I believe that there are signs to suggest that we are in those last days. God is doing amazing and miraculous things all across the globe, but the devil is also very active, catching many in his cruel and destructive vice. Even Christians can be deceived by his cunning schemes, as he offers detours that seem attractive but actually bring those fooled by him into bondage and doubt, causing them to miss out on God's best for their lives. We must be alert and constantly on our guard. Claiming ignorance is no excuse.

I find there is a distinct reluctance among Christians today to talk about the devil. I have noticed people visibly switching off and looking uncomfortable at the mere mention of Satan, as if all such conversations should be avoided and we should only talk about the good things that are happening in the world. I admit that I used to think the same. I felt that too much attention was given to him and that, as he is a nobody, we need not give him a second thought. During the last few years, however, I have come to realize that this is exactly what the devil wants us to think. Jesus was confronted by the devil many times during His earthly ministry. He talked to the devil, He rebuked the devil, but He also totally overcame the devil, sometimes by quoting the Word of God. There is a very powerful scripture in Revelation that says, 'For the accuser of our brothers, who accuses them before our

God day and night, has been hurled down. They overcame him by the blood of the Lamb and by the word of
their testimony' (Revelation 12:10b-11a).

Christians should not fall into the trap of believing
that the devil can do us no harm, that he is not interested
in us and that he is unable to destroy us, because it is a lie.
The powers of darkness do exist and we have to remember that there are two spiritual forces in the world – good
and bad, light and darkness. Evidence for both is in abundance within the pages of the Bible, and indeed throughout the world.

The devil is a defeated foe, and the battle has already
been won at Calvary. The devil's destiny is waiting for
him – there is no doubt as to his ultimate future – and he
knows it. There is no salvation for him, and he knows that
too. Yet he also knows that every Christian has the potential to live the victorious, abundant life that Jesus has
promised, and his job is to blind our eyes so that we cannot see all the wonderful things God has for us. If we give
Satan an inch, he will take a mile. Just as water finds a
hairline crack in a vessel, so he will find any weakness that
believers have, which has not been handed over to God.
If we are aware of this, we should also know how to avoid
the danger. The Bible is a living book, and the truths contained in it are more than able to set us free. If we are
obedient to God and walk in His ways, we hamper the
devil's devices and make it difficult for him to touch us.
Satan cannot win if we walk in obedience to the pattern
for living which the Lord has lovingly given us.

God is faithful

Although people often think that divorce is a situation that affects only two people, the husband and wife, in most cases it is something that greatly affects the whole family, even when the children of the marriage are adults and married themselves. Everyone struggles to understand what has happened and to take on board the implications for the future.

I found that every member of my family was thrown into emotional turmoil as they endeavoured to cope with the situation, which obviously took on a different form for each one and was changing by the day. On several occasions, it did seem that more splits in the family were about to happen and there was a time when I wondered whether we would ever relate properly as a family again. I also knew that the devil targets relationships and that the only way to triumph over him was to surrender the whole situation to God, even though things looked pretty grim and hopeless.

It is certainly not easy to praise God when trouble and strife are present and there seems to be no way out. I knew, however, that to obey God in this area was our only hope as a family. When we give people and situations over to God and allow Him to lead us, He walks with us every step of the way and carries us through some of the most difficult terrain, just as He has promised and as 2 Timothy 1:12a indicates: 'For I know whom I have believed, and am persuaded that he is able to keep that which I have committed unto him against that day' (KJV).

He has done great things

Today, although my situation is still all fairly fresh and new, I can testify that God has done great things in my life and for my family, and that He has been like a strong tower into which we have been able to run and be safe during the worst of the storm. In spite of being newly divorced, I now have a contentment and real peace that I am confident only God Himself is able to give.

God is so faithful and knows just what and who we need at any given time. I believe, through personal experience, that He is able to bring the right people into our lives and across our paths at the exactly the right moments. Some may be lifelong friends, while others with whom He causes us to rub shoulders are maybe there just for a season. These dear people, who I believe are divinely appointed by God, cannot fail to influence and mould our characters. I am so very grateful to God for all the wonderful people He has put beside me, who have encouraged, mentored and helped me during my lifetime and especially over the last few years.

After Bob left I felt that, for security purposes, the house needed to be inhabited at all times. It became an increasingly urgent matter for me to find someone to live in, preferably a married couple, to give me some degree of protection and also to enable me to travel and leave the house without having to engage housesitters each time. Finding the right person or people presented me with a very daunting task. Having people to live in your home is a decision that should never be entered into lightly, as there will undoubtedly be many challenges to overcome. The people who fill that role should certainly be God-appointed.

Keith and Yvonne Lee were the good folk God gave me to fill that need. Once again, boundaries had to be made which protected their privacy and mine, and which had to be adhered to if the relationship was to work in the manner for which it was intended. I thank God for Keith and Yvonne, who fit perfectly into that position. They have their own quarters within the house, giving them the space that they both need and deserve. Having them around has been such a blessing, and the arrangement seems to work extremely well. I guess it will only be for a season, but I am praying that it will be a long and happy one. They are a Christian couple, in ministry, who love the Lord and have much the same desire as myself to see the Kingdom of God extended and people released into their destiny in God.

Being alone seems to send shock waves through some people; they are horrified even at the thought of it. I have to say, however, that I now quite enjoy the times when I am entirely alone – which is not very often, given that I have a family who live very close and grandchildren who live next door. I also greatly enjoy the times when the family are all together, maybe for Sunday lunch, when chaos reigns! When I think of my family and my friends, I feel I am rich indeed.

A greater kind of wealth

We tend to measure our worth by our worldly goods and cash in the bank, but there is a far greater wealth which is within everyone's reach. God has given us His standards to live by. At one time they were the basis by which the law was framed in Britain, but now they are not even known by many of the younger generation. Nonetheless, they give a pattern for how we are to relate to God and our fellow human beings. Although they were given to Moses by God several thousands of years ago, they have still to be bettered by anything we humans can come up with. And, although it is impossible to keep the Commandments in our own strength, they do at least give a guideline for us to press towards, causing us to come into a much greater wealth than that which we can gain by sweat and toil. Obedience to God is a kind of regulator that causes blessings to flow, which in turn brings a deep-down peace, a sense of one's own worth, and a security which is based on the relationship we have with our Heavenly Father.

Now that is wealth that no one can possibly cheat us out of or steal from us. That is true wealth, and it will bring us the great joy and security in life that many think money alone can bring. If we teach the importance of these principles to our children, we will leave them a legacy far more valuable than anything we might have in the bank when we die. If they learn to live by those principles, they will prosper in all ways, and their obedience will bring peace, health and happiness to every area of their lives as they grow in wisdom and in the ways of the Lord.

You might be thinking that you can never be happy again, due to the things that have gone on in your life. I know only too well what it is to feel that way. In the next chapter, however, I want to share with you how an ordinary plane journey reminded me of an exciting and liberating spiritual truth – and how that truth can transform lives, including yours.

ELEVEN

Nothing too hard for God

One rather dull March day, as Debbie and I boarded the plane at Heathrow on our way to attend a women's conference in Sydney, Australia, I noticed that the sky was very dark and thundery. As the plane took off, I comforted myself with the fact that at least we were guaranteed lots of blue sky and warm sunshine at our destination. As it turned out, however, we did not have to wait that long.

Moments after the plane was airborne, we started to fly above the clouds and into the most perfect summer's day. Here was the blue sky and warm sunshine that I had envisaged at the other end of the journey. Dark grey clouds were obliterating the sky and stopping the people below from experiencing it, but as our plane began to break through those clouds, we were able to enjoy a much better deal. The sun was streaming into the plane because the clouds were beneath us. They had not dispersed, they were still there as black and threatening as ever, but we were above and beyond where they were, looking down upon them. It was certainly a very different world up there, with the bright light and warmth from the sunshine making everything in the aircraft sparkle and gleam, including the faces of our fellow passengers.

As I settled down in my seat, with many flying hours stretching before me, I took a peak out of the window at the picturesque view and started to think how like the Christian life this flight was. It is God's will for every one of us to be able to soar into heavenly places. He desires to take us into realms we could never dream of, and could certainly never reach in our own strength. Yet sometimes, because of the circumstances that surround us and because we tend to live by our feelings and not by faith, we miss all the goodies that God has lovingly prepared for us.

Every airline pilot is trained to fly by what his instruments tell him in bad weather and when visibility is down to zero. He has to rely on his instruments to get him through the storm safely. He must not, even for a moment, disbelieve the readings from his instruments, regardless of his instincts, because sometimes the G-forces can play nasty tricks and tell a totally different story. His rigorous training will have taught him to ignore what he feels and put his whole trust in the instruments before him. If he takes his eyes off them for one moment, he could very easily become totally disorientated, with disastrous effects. Eventually, his persistence pays off as he breaks through the cloud and is able to see clearly once again.

Many times in the pages of this book I have emphasized that things are not always what they seem and that we must put our faith and whole trust in God and His Word, and walk in the way He directs us. The Bible tells us that we must walk by faith and not by sight. The way may seem to be in total opposition to how we think or feel, and we may not be able to see a way out of our present circumstances – but God can, and if we fix our eyes on Him, He will guide us out of harm's way into safe and secure pastures. When we receive Jesus into our lives, we come into a new and personal relationship with Him that is totally alien to the way we have been living in the past. It is as if a light has suddenly been turned on, or as if we have just come out of thick cloud and into the glorious sunshine.

Beyond understanding

It is often said that 'there's no place like home', and I second that. The time that I am able to spend at home and with my family is for me the part of my life that I really and truly enjoy most. Home is where I really love to be. Yet I have also been fortunate enough to journey to every continent in the world, time and time again, and I still do so, maybe even more now than I did before. I also very much enjoy all this travel, especially when there is a special purpose for my journey. The fact that I now sometimes have cause to travel completely alone never really bothers me.

I believe that the secret of my contentment, whether at home or away, is both simple and exciting. God has given me, true to His promise, a peace that passes all understanding. I find it impossible to put into words. Occasionally I feel guilty that I feel so whole and together after such a traumatic experience as divorce. After all, divorce turns your life upside down and usually takes a terrible toll on those who experience it unwillingly. I sometimes feel that maybe I should still be licking my wounds and tending to my scars after such an awful experience – but amazingly I am not!

I realize that there are people who have experienced far worse trials and tribulations than I have, as divorce is sadly commonplace these days – but the emotional side is very similar, whatever trauma comes our way. The good news is that, when we choose to commit our way to the Lord, He is more than able to protect us and turn the whole situation around for His glory and honour, and also for our blessing. He has never made a mess of anyone's life, and He is not going to start with mine, or yours! Nonetheless, we have to choose to trust Him to carry us through the very darkest times and the cloudiest of days, until we are able to break through those angry clouds and into the clear blue sky.

As you have read my story, you may well have thought that, since everything seems to have worked out all right for me, maybe it was God's will that Bob and I divorced. I do not believe that to be true for one minute. The God we serve is a God of restoration and unity, and His intention is not to tear couples apart or divide families. He is a God of order, and He gives us guidelines to live by. These include guidelines on married life, and if we all chose to obey them there would certainly be no need for divorce. When we acknowledge Him in all our ways and give our inadequacies and failures to Him who is our only hope, He is able to use those situations, however bad, for our good and will 'restore to us all the years the locusts have eaten' (Joel 2:25). God's heart is to revive, not destroy.

The life that Jesus promises and longs to give us is full to the very brim and running over with good things. Jesus said, 'I am the bread of life. Eat of me and you will never hunger,' and, 'Come unto me all you that are thirsty and you will never thirst again' (John 6:35). Just as we cannot live without eating and drinking, so we cannot afford to reject Him: He is as vital to us as food and drink. Even in the valley experiences, when all around is black and dismal, when trials come and knock us off our feet, and even when our friends fail and perhaps even desert us, we can know that He is with us every moment of every day. We do not have to feel lonely or in despair. As we take His hand and allow Him to walk beside us, we can have an inner peace and an abundant joy that defies all reason.

Happiness is only dependent on happenings, circumstances and possessions – but joy, the real, lasting joy that Jesus gives, is constantly bubbling up within, even during the darkest times. We may not feel happy sometimes, because of the things that are happening around us, but we can at the same time feel full of joy deep down, because we know, without a shadow of a doubt, who we are in Christ as we establish a close relationship with Him. He is our friend, one who sticks closer than a brother and who will never fail us or let us down. Once we have asked Him into our hearts and lives, He proves Himself to us and His promises become a reality. There is no doubt, the Christian life is the most exciting and fulfilling life by far. The Bible sums it up in this way: 'I have set before you life and death, blessings and curses. Now choose life, so that you and your children may live . . .' (Deuteronomy 30:19).

Some people take a casual glance at Christianity and start to feel sorry for Christians, thinking that they live a restricted and boring life. How clever the lies of Satan are, because in fact the very opposite is true. The Christian life is the very best life that anyone can possibly live, offering abundant joy and a peace that is not dependent on past or present circumstances, possessions or wealth. Sometimes people are confused by those they have encountered who are religious but have no personal relationship with God. That kind of person is sometimes wrongly identified as a born-again believer, reinforcing the myth that the Christian life is dull and prohibitive. Fortunately for us, Jesus has promised, 'I have come that they may have life, and that they may have it more abundantly' (John 10:10 NKJV).

Our will or God's?

One of the reasons why I believe divorce is widespread today and increasingly accepted as normal, with many couples hardly grieving when faced with it, is that many of them married with the thought that they *could* divorce one another if the going got tough and the marriage proved to be too difficult. It takes two to get married, but unfortunately only one to initiate a divorce. We say our vows on our wedding day, when of course both bride and groom are present, but when a couple divorce neither party has to attend court while a judge stamps a piece of paper, ending the marriage. He possibly never gives a moment's thought to what the Bible says about the act he has carried out. Under our legal system, however, what the civil courts decree is final.

From childhood I was aware of what the Bible says on the subject of divorce, and down the years I saw much heartache and suffering caused by marriage breakdown. I knew when I married that, as far as I was concerned, marriage was for life – there was never any doubt in my mind about that.

When men or women go off with someone else, they very often tell their new partner that their marriage has been dead for a long time, that the relationship with their spouse is nonexistent and that they have been sleeping in separate beds for months or even years – because they fear that if they do not say that, the new person in their life will not stick around for very long. And, I suppose in order to give them hope for the future, they also say that they intend to divorce their wife or husband as soon as they can. This is rarely the case, however, and very often the real truth is that they quite simply enjoy having the best of both worlds.

In our case, Bob and I lived in every respect as a married couple until the day he suddenly left. We never once slept in separate beds or rooms. Of course, the last months that we spent together were not particularly good times because, as you can imagine, there was something of a tug of war going on. Yet Bob was a good husband and I never once doubted that he was the one God lovingly put beside me for all those years. I certainly know that God did not tear us apart and that it was not His will for us as a family to suffer such pain and suffering. That was, once again, mainly the result of choices made by us – not only by Bob, but sadly by me too. I also know that God does not – in fact cannot – go back on His Word, which states that He hates divorce (Malachi 2:16). He did not suddenly decide that, because our marriage had run into difficulties after 30 years, it would be best for us to part. God is a God of the supernatural – nothing is too hard for Him. Nonetheless, because of the choices we are allowed to make in life, we sometimes find ourselves on a very different and unfamiliar road – one that has the potential to make us live far below the standard that God intended for us.

I have heard it said that some divorces are like abortions: while the marriage still has some life in it, it is terminated. Many people are totally against abortion and would actively campaign to bring it to an end, but they think nothing about finishing a marriage that is perhaps only a little stale, a term that could be used to describe most marriages at some time or another. Those same marriages can become like new if both sides allow God to breathe life into them once again. Remember, nothing is too hard for God.

'Train up a child . . .'

The book of Proverbs has some good advice: 'Pay attention to what I say; listen closely to my words. Do not let them out of your sight, keep them within your heart; for they are life to those who find them and health to a man's whole body. Above all else, guard your heart, for it is the wellspring of life' (Proverbs 4:20-23). Although these words were written many hundreds of years ago, they are still as relevant today as ever they were. We ignore their wisdom at our peril.

This is something I have tried to teach my children over the years. All three are now married to Christian partners and have homes of their own, and I know that God has a great and exciting life planned for them too. For the last five years Andrew and Alison have lived in the house next door, which is still a car ride away, and they have produced for us four lovely granddaughters.

Andrew works in his father's business, IM Group Limited of West Bromwich, the same company that Bob began to build in his late twenties. They now not only import Subaru and various other cars, including Daihatsu, but in the last 10 years the firm has also branched out into the property market. The company is thriving and growing year by year, and Andrew, who is managing director of Daihatsu, loves his job and has proved to be a great asset to the company.

Debbie is married to Matthew, the son of a pastor from Sutton Coldfield, and, like her sister, has not produced any offspring as yet. Matthew also works for Subaru, and Debbie is a fully qualified hairdresser. Until recently Debbie owned her own salon, which at one point was voted one of the top five in the area.

Angela, married to Noel, works at Bedworth Christian Centre as PA to the pastors and their wives, and loves being part of the team that deals with the general running of her church. Noel, meanwhile, has recently started his own internet design company.

All my children attend the church at Bedworth and are involved in some way or other in its many activities. It is great to see them week by week praising and worshipping God, and to watch them growing spiritually and getting to know God for themselves. I know that they all have their different challenges and things they will have to work through with God's help, but I thank God for them and commit them into His care each day, thanking Him for the wonderful blessing they have been to us. The three of them, together with their spouses, are very good friends and often the six of them go out together. It is magnificent to see this, as they love each other dearly and there is not one ounce of rivalry between them.

I do not feel that I have been an exceptional parent in any way, and I know that Bob would join me in saying the same about himself. In fact, we have both been known to be rather inconsistent at times concerning our children's upbringing, as is probably the case with many parents. As anyone in that role knows, it is a continual learning process. Yet, when we commit our offspring to the Lord, which is without doubt the wisest action we can possibly take, we can rest in the assurance that our insufficiencies become His sufficiencies.

As I look back on my own childhood, I feel very grateful to my parents for the way they brought me up. They sacrificed many things for me. Sometimes we do not realize until we are much older just how much our parents did for us. As they were both in their forties when I was born, they were, much to my embarrassment as a youngster, often mistaken for my grandparents. Nonetheless, I believe that their somewhat Victorian values proved to be a blessing rather than a hindrance in my life. As I mentioned in an earlier chapter, they both found the Lord in a genuine way – my father just days before he died. My mother was a widow for 26 years before she died at the age of 88. She suffered from Alzheimer's disease, but died peacefully in her bed and now I know, without a shadow of a doubt, that she is with the Lord.

I have also been very blessed with wonderful in-laws. I have already mentioned that my father-in-law was killed very suddenly in a car crash in August 1977. I remember being terribly sad at his passing, almost as if he were my own father, as we had a good relationship and I was extremely fond of him. My mother-in-law was left as a widow at the age of 56. As I write, she will be turning 80 in a few weeks' time, and she does not look a day over 65! She has attended a Catholic church all her life, and I know that her faithful example and many prayers down the years could not have failed to have a big impact on the family. We have had a 35-year relationship, and I still refer to her as 'Mum'. She is a very dear and prominent member of my family, and a wonderful grandmother to my children and great-grandmother to my grandchildren. Nothing can ever change that. Bob and I were both blessed with parents who not only cared for us but also taught us by example how to lead upright and honest lives.

Wise parents begin to train and teach their children from the very beginning, to prepare them for the day when they will be self-sufficient and responsible adults, able to make good decisions about every aspect of their lives. Sometimes, however, the more input parents have had into their children's lives, the harder they find it when the children finally leave home. Their departure can leave the parents feeling redundant, with a great deal of time up ahead and not much to fill it. This is often the moment when marriages begin to develop cracks and fall apart, as mine did.

The truth of the matter is that this is actually a time when God can bless and enrich a couple who have been good and faithful parents, by allowing them to move on into further areas of ministry where the talents they have employed as parents can be used and appreciated in a different way. It is certainly not His plan for couples to renounce their marriage bonds once their parental duties are over. Many married couples, once their children are off their hands, go on to do mighty things for God, often in other countries and in places to which they never even dreamt they would travel. Others are content to stay in their home country, but find great fulfilment in the latter years of their lives as they take up a whole new set of interests and allow the relationship, which may have lost its way a little, to be developed and enriched.

We do not have to struggle and strive if we have sown good seeds: when harvest time comes, it is relatively easy. 'For my yoke is easy and my burden is light' (Matthew 11:29). Any farmer will tell you that the most difficult time is just before the harvest, and the Bible tells us that we will reap if we faint not, and that we are to 'press toward the mark for the prize of the high calling of God in Christ Jesus' (Philippians 3:14 KJV). Sometimes the best is yet to come – in fact, it is possibly just around the next bend in the road, but perhaps we have had so many nasty bends leading up to this point that we bail out and abandon the journey just as we are about to reach our final destination. Just like the pilot: if he were to mistrust his instruments and take his eyes off them for one moment, he could come crashing down and never reach his destination. Those who are winners and cross the finishing line are those who absolutely refuse to quit.

Abundant life

I suppose I could now be classed as 'single', or 'single again'. Yet I do not actually feel single, as I have in-laws, three wonderful children and several grandchildren, and single people do not normally have those blessings! I have had all the comforts and benefits of a long and happy marriage, and yet now I am single and have all the many advantages that go with that. I am free to serve God and constantly look to Him for guidance and direction. He is the most faithful husband that anyone can have. There are so many good things about being in this position, and I have no regrets whatsoever. If I had my life over again, I would make very few changes. In fact, I hope I can say with Paul, 'I have learned to be content whatever the circumstances. I know what it is to be in need, and I know what it is to have plenty. I have learned the secret of being content in any and every situation' (Philippians 4:11).

I am not clever, talented or gifted in any one particular area – in fact, I have always considered myself as a bit of a jack of all trades but master of none. I am fully aware that in myself I can do nothing, but I also know that I can do all things through Him who gives me the power. He is the strength of my life: without Him I would surely fail. Without God and His Word, in fact, I would be a hopeless case.

During the last few years I have found it necessary on more than one occasion to meet on a business level with several people in the secular world – an undertaking totally outside my comfort zone. I now have a financial adviser, several lawyers, accountants and many others who all offer me wise counsel, and there have been occasions when I have had working lunches in the City of London in order to discuss financial affairs that used to be handled by Bob. On one occasion I almost dissolved into giggles as I sat at a table in a posh London restaurant with five business advisers, all of whom were using technical jargon that went straight over my head. I remember thinking, 'If only Bob could see me now!' I must add, though, that I am learning, and many things that Bob had to deal with in this area obviously rubbed off on me in some way, as I hear myself sometimes dealing with matters in exactly the same way that Bob himself would have done. I have tried to keep business matters to the very minimum, as they can be very time consuming, but at the same time I realize that God expects us to be good stewards of the gifts He has bestowed upon us.

During the last couple of years, the road of my life has obviously been somewhat rocky, and I have had to overcome many difficult, unfamiliar and painful patches. Yet I feel today that I have come into a much richer and deeper relationship with God. I know that He accepts me in spite of my many faults and failings. I may have failed, but I know that I am not a failure in His eyes. Sometimes we bestow that label upon ourselves out of guilt and condemnation, and even proceed to carry the shame with us through life – but I know that I am special to God, even though I fail Him constantly, and I know that, as I allow God to continue to mould me, He will make me into a whole and beautiful person for Himself.

I have a long way to go yet – I am still on the potter's wheel, so to speak – but I am confident that He has a wonderful destiny for my life and all those years have certainly not been wasted. God is for me, not against me. He saw fit to die for me, and I know that all I am today is due to nothing that I have done, but is entirely due to the marvellous grace and everlasting faithfulness of God.

That in no way makes me a cut above the rest. Everyone reading this has exactly the same chances as I do, and so does everyone else on this planet. We are all equal in God: He does not have favourites. We do not have to make ourselves good enough before we call upon Him. We are able to come into His presence just as we are, with all our shortcomings. God is our Father, and He wants us to come to Him with all our faults and failings because He died for every single one of us, warts and all. We all have exactly the same chances and choices to make. We can choose to make those bridges of gold, allowing the things that would torment us to depart, releasing us into the fullness that Jesus obtained for us on the cross. We can choose life, or we can choose death. The choice is ours.

Do I need to be married to become a whole person and to fulfil my God-given destiny? The answer to that is a definite 'no'. I am gradually learning to be content in the new and unusual situation in which I now find myself. And although my marriage – which I treasured and considered a very precious gift from God – did not quite make it, I thank God that because of His wondrous grace, mercy and never-ending love, and because no weapon formed against me can possibly prosper, I did!

TWELVE

Water into wine

Although this is the concluding chapter of the book, I know that it is certainly not the end of the story. That is something I am more than happy to leave entirely in God's divinely capable hands. Just like everyone else on this planet, my life continues to evolve and expand, and I am constantly amazed at the situations and responsibilities with which God trusts me, in spite of the fact that I still have so much more to learn about Him and His ways.

The Bible is an all-powerful, life-changing book and I have known from my youth that, if obeyed, it has the answers to my every problem and trial, every addiction and character defect, every bad habit and trait. Ironically, over the years I have on more than one occasion spoken at meetings on the importance of the Bible, saying that it is not just a boring old book gathering dust on a shelf, but that it has a life-changing message for all who take the trouble to obey its teachings, offering the answer to every trouble and hardship. During the last few years, I found myself having to put into practice all that I had previously preached.

Due to the turmoil in my mind and all the activity that was taking place in my life while my marriage was falling apart, I found I had great difficulty in sleeping and dreaded going to bed at night. In order to take my mind off my problems, I would lie in bed consciously quoting Scripture – every verse I could think of, over and over again as I lay in the dark, passage after passage, including some that I had hidden in my heart since my childhood. It helped to keep me from constantly thinking about a situation which did not seem to make sense, and to which there seemed to be no answer or way out – a situation that was causing me to become extremely tearful and depressed.

Long before the break-up, I had been listening to teaching tapes from the ministries of Gary Whetstone, John Maxwell, John Bevere and many others, and had been greatly blessed as many fresh revelations and truths were unfolded to me. I now found myself listening to tapes by the score, soaking up their messages like a sponge, mostly at night after turning off the light. Christian television was only available in the mornings in those days, so most evenings, as I sat at home alone, I would turn to the Bible in desperation and sit devouring large parts of it. Sometimes, believe me, it was the last thing I felt like doing – but then again, I did not much like feeling depressed, defeated and in utter despair either. I knew deep down that the Word had power to change my situation, my heart and my life, and each time I disciplined myself to read it I felt my spirit lifting, my depression receding, and the Lord very close to me.

Looking back now, I believe that I was force-feeding myself with anything of a biblical nature that I could get hold of and that I felt might benefit me, in order to deaden the agonizing pain I was experiencing inside. I knew that the Bible and the message it contained had the power and authority to see me through absolutely any situation, and the dreadful predicament in which I found myself was no exception. Isaiah 55:11 is a clear statement from God concerning the Word that proceeds from His mouth: 'It shall not return unto me void, but it shall accomplish that which I please, and it shall prosper in the thing whereto I sent it' (KJV).

Gradually, over the weeks and months, my attitude and thinking started to alter in a remarkable way. I was steadily changing – and I knew it. God had been so faithful to me in the past and I knew that He would not fail me now, but would continue to be all that He had promised to be. There were, of course, good days and bad days, and days when I simply felt numb and wondered if it was really worth all the effort. Then gradually, as His Word began to take root in my heart, I was aware that the good days were beginning to outweigh the bad. Life in general became far less distressing and traumatic as I took each day as it came, knowing that God had brought me this far and would certainly be with me to help me complete my journey to wholeness.

Little by little I began to grow stronger, more positive and more hopeful. I can truthfully say that I physically felt the presence of God with me as each moment passed. I give God all the glory and honour for His faithfulness and love to me during that incredibly difficult time. The Lord's promise is that He will be with us always and in every situation, and when I was at my very lowest point, God met me in a wonderful way. The problems still existed, but it seemed that God was pulling me through, to a higher place, with His strong and mighty Hand.

A burden for others

Emotional pain and adversity, given to God and dealt with according to God's Word, can leave a stamp upon the survivor that is sweet and gentle and enables them to minister to and enrich the lives of others, making them a blessing to all those with whom they come into contact.

My own situation caused me to think about many people I knew who were also going through extremely difficult times, or had done so in the past. We all know the principle of cause and effect, sowing and reaping – but what about those circumstances that just seem to come out of the blue, randomly hitting those who happen to be around? What about earthquakes and floods, or an innocent child being knocked down by a drunken driver, or cancer suddenly striking a young mum with children who still need her love and care? What are we to think when bad things happen to good people? I fell to wondering if the Bible had an answer for that kind of circumstance too.

Then I remembered the story in Matthew 13 that Jesus told about the tares and the wheat. Under the cover of darkness, while people were asleep, an enemy sowed darnel into the newly planted wheat. Darnel, which in the Bible is also referred to as 'tares', is a plant that looks very much like wheat when it first pushes its way out of the ground. By the time it comes to maturity, however, it has developed quite distinct characteristics – which is just as well, because if its seed is mixed in with the corn, the resulting flour is poisonous. Recognizing the seriousness of the deed, the servant responsible for the field quite understandably wanted to do something about it immediately, and was probably very surprised when the owner of the field told him to do absolutely nothing, at least for the time being. Why? Well, the owner knew that at this early stage of the crop's life, even the most experienced farmer would have great difficulty knowing which was wheat and which was darnel. Yet he also knew that time would solve the problem for him, if everyone had the patience and faith to wait. He knew that by the time the plants were ready to harvest, the black-seeded, poisonous darnel would be standing erect against the blue sky, while the wheat stalks would be bowed down under their nutritious and life-sustaining load. At this point the plants would be easily distinguishable and could be safely taken from the field, the tares to be gathered in bundles and thrown on the fire, the wheat to be carefully stored in the master's barn.

Instead of dealing with difficult situations our way, we sometimes need to be patient and let those apparently impossible situations come to maturity. God has all eternity to put right the injustices that have taken place, and He will do it in His time and in His way. 'There is nothing concealed that will not be disclosed, or hidden that will not be made known' (Luke 12:2).

Going through the breakdown of my relationship with Bob and the subsequent divorce was a very painful, difficult and traumatic experience, even though I had God's help. Deep down in my spirit I knew that my only hope was to trust God and cast my care upon Him, knowing that He would not fail to bring me through. I knew that God's promise was that He would deliver all those who trust in Him from all – yes, all – their trials and tribulations, and that He could even turn those disasters into victories. Knowing this to be a truth that brings freedom, I began to have a burden for those who were living with emotional baggage, victims of past mistakes and misfortunes with no idea at all that it was possible to walk in total freedom from those things and live a joyful life without shame and condemnation. So many did not know the principles and patterns that God Himself has laid down, which ensure that we are able to recover from any hardship as a better person and begin walking in the liberty that Jesus died so that we might have.

Just like Shadrach, Meshach and Abednego, who were thrown into a fiery furnace but were protected by God so that only their bonds were burnt and they emerged not even smelling of smoke, I had an overwhelming desire to tell those I met that they too could come out of their fiery trials without the stench of their situation clinging to them. I felt, even in the midst of my own emotional chaos, that God was telling me to abandon my tendency to stand in the shadows and to do something positive about this, instead of just thinking about it and waiting for someone else to put the wheels in motion.

Equipping for freedom

As I prayed about the things I was feeling, my thinking began to centre on the formation of some sort of ministry or foundation that would fully equip people, maybe even those already in ministry, to be able to lead to freedom all those who were bound and captive, by putting powerful biblical principles into practice as Jesus taught us to. I realized that it is quite possible to be a Christian for many years without living a victorious life, and without truly understanding the ways of God. Many people, I realized, were spiritually dying because of lack of knowledge of the life-giving Word of God. I believe that God wants all of us, whoever we are, to adopt a teachable spirit at all times, as there are always new truths to be learned that can in turn be passed on to nurture the lives of others. It is never too late, and we are never too old to learn new things. In fact, the moment we stop learning is the moment we begin to stagnate. However fresh water is, if it does not keep flowing, it will eventually lose its freshness and become pungent and stale. The Bible speaks about the River of God, which is full of movement and life.

Apart from further equipping and empowering those who already knew the Lord, I felt that we also needed to reach out to others with the life-changing message of the gospel, which had been such a powerful and influential part of my life since I was a child. I have, after all, been on both sides of the fence: I know what it is to feel rejected, lonely and empty inside, trying to make sense of the world, but I also know what it is like to experience the love of God streaming into my heart, making me feel clean and whole, and giving me the strength to face situations that previously had been far too big and complex for me to handle. I started to discover what many Christians had realized throughout the ages – that once we have a relationship with Jesus, we do not have to wait until we die to experience the joys and blessings of heaven. Just like the Children of Israel after leaving the bondage of Egypt, we immediately begin to experience the joy and fulfilment of walking with God on a daily basis.

Down the years, I have had the thrill of seeing many members of my family come to know the Lord personally. I have seen their lives change before my very eyes. I watched the wonderful gospel message of salvation touch my mother, giving her a peace and joy which had eluded her in her earlier years. Then I was able to witness my father's attitude to life change after he had asked Jesus into his heart, giving him a peace and calmness that he had never really had before, even though he only had a few days to live. I also saw how the love of God transformed Bob when he was a teenager, giving him an overwhelming desire to serve God and to reach out to those in need, often to his own personal cost. Then gradually, other key members of Bob's family – including his brother Mike and sister-in-law Barbara, and his sister Viv – had all come to the point of giving their lives to Jesus. Even Viv's husband Adolf, who died when he was only 51, found the Lord in the last few months of his life. As my own children began to grow, I saw the gospel message touch their lives too, keeping them free from the excesses in which so many of their generation sadly became entangled, and turning them into loving, caring adults.

With the evidence of these transformed lives in front of me, I knew that Christianity is much more than a philosophy or the ability to keep a set of rules. It is a living, dynamic faith – a relationship with the resurrected Jesus, who is as alive today as when He walked and talked with His disciples 2,000 years ago, and who is just as able to save and heal as He was then. My own relationship with Him touched every part of my life, every day, and increasingly became something that I wanted to share with everyone I met. I knew that the gospel message was too good to keep to myself, and that the Word of God has the power to change anyone and everyone. I began to wonder what might be achieved if a training centre could be established that would allow for such teaching, where believers could openly and honestly share their experiences with each other, and where those attending could become thoroughly grounded and built up in the Word of God.

As the idea took shape in my mind, I realized afresh that I had a unique opportunity to use the resources at my disposal for the Kingdom of God. I had discovered many years before the glorious truth that whatever we give to Him will not go unnoticed. As when Jesus fed the 5,000 with just five small loaves and two fish, it seems that He always gives back in abundance in one way or another. I was excited about all that could be achieved if the vision that He had given me to fulfil could be realized.

Release Foundation

The outworking of that vision was the creation of Release Foundation, which was founded as a vehicle to encourage, empower and motivate others to get on with the important task I believe God wants to undertake in all our lives. Why did we choose the name Release? Well, it implies freedom, lack of bondage and the ability to do and be all that we were originally created for – which is what God brings into the lives of all those who come to Him and choose to follow His ways. Our aim is to release spiritual giants into our land who in turn are able to empower and commission others to aspire to higher levels with God. Release is a charitable trust that seeks to help people of all ages, cultures and spiritual backgrounds to realize their full potential in Jesus. It comes under the spiritual covering of my own Fellowship in Bedworth.

What we certainly do not wish to do is to pump Christians with yet more information and head knowledge. At Release we believe that it is vitally important to disciple and equip those who are eager to become actively involved in the work of the Lord and who show leadership qualities of any kind, so that they are able to present the truth of the Christian message in a way that is spiritually dynamic, culturally relevant and personally applicable, while at the same time displaying the fruit of the Spirit in their own lives. We are fully aware that it is impossible to impart to others what we do not possess ourselves.

I firmly believe that the character and quality of staff is a vitally important issue in any organization, especially where God's work is concerned. God has very graciously raised up some excellent people to join the team at Release. Among others, we are really blessed to have Chris Spicer as the Director of Studies. He is the one responsible for the curriculum and the selection of speakers to lecture on different topics applicable to each course. Chris is the uncle of my pastor Gary, and is an anointed pastor and excellent Bible teacher. He is in charge of most of the activities of the training school itself. We are also privileged to have the services of Ralph Coleman as Administrator. He does an excellent job and is 100 per cent behind the vision God has given us. Although I am a trustee and endeavour to ensure that the centre is run effectively and the God-given vision carried out, I am not personally involved in the day-to-day running of the activities of Release.

We run a variety of courses for a wide range of people who want to learn more about being effective in their service for God. The courses offer advice and training on subjects as diverse as worship and mentoring. Some are held just over a weekend, while others are long-term projects in which the candidates can involve themselves over several months, without having to visit the centre personally.

One of the courses closest to my heart is, unsurprisingly, one that helps married couples. We have a special burden for the spiritual health of couples and marriages in general, and with that in mind we felt that it would be of great benefit to the Kingdom of God to hold 'marriage enrichment' weekends from time to time. The first one, which took place as I started to write this chapter, proved to be a very valuable, empowering and enjoyable time for all who attended.

I believe we are living in days when Christian marriages especially are under severe attack, as divorce defies many scriptural principles laid down by God Himself and brings heartache and chaos into the lives of many. It is a sad fact that broken relationships are an everyday occurrence, even in Christian circles. How awesome it would be to see many broken relationships healed by the power of God, marriages enriched and renewed instead of torn apart, couples renewing their commitment to one another and to God. Knowing that other marriages were being repaired, although mine failed, would be the icing on the cake as far as I am concerned. It would prove that what the devil intended for bad, God can, without doubt, turn around for good. God is a God of unity, reconciliation and restoration, and I am sure that each marriage relationship that is restored and enriched brings great pleasure to God's heart.

We have had some excellent feedback from those who have been on the courses we have held so far, but we are always looking for ways in which they can be improved. Our desire is to assist and impact those whose lives we touch in the most effective way possible.

Not very long after Release Foundation was formed, we were offered the yacht *Genevieve* and realized with delight that she could be another means of carrying out our vision. The various programmes in which the yacht is now involved are just as exciting as the courses back at our UK base. The idea is to use *Genevieve* as a training base for Christians from all denominations and walks of life, as well as a centre for evangelism as she sails in the Mediterranean.

We are fortunate indeed to have secured the services of Christian skipper Theo Goutzios and his wife Sandra, who are committed to the project for at least the next five years. Theo is of Greek descent, but actually comes from Australia. He and his wife, who oversees the general running of the yacht, are a very godly couple and share our desire to see lives changed. They are both very caring people, and they go out of their way to ensure that the needs of all who step aboard are catered for and that they are made to feel very welcome. Theo is also a Bible teacher and mentor and is able to share his wisdom and experience with those who come aboard. Our other skipper, Cameron, has excellent technical skills, and his knowledge in this area has already been a great benefit to the ministry.

In the year 2000, our first year of operation, over 250 people came aboard *Genevieve*, meeting with other Christians from different parts of the world as well as sharing their experiences and praying with each other. At the beginning of October 2000 I spent a week on board in my capacity as a trustee, and met with some of our own Bedworth missionaries who are presently working in Albania. We spent a fantastic few days together. Several other missionaries from different parts of the world were also on board, enjoying a well-earned rest from their normal surroundings and ministerial activities. Facilities are very good and, once a few minor alterations have taken place this winter, will soon be even better. The food is both delicious and plentiful, and those I spoke to on board were very reluctant to leave at the end of their stay! We all found that the relaxed and happy atmosphere of the ship caused us to open up our hearts to each other, producing great interaction. People left at the end of the week knowing they were different from when they arrived.

That is what the work of *Genevieve* is all about. Although so far she has only been used during the summer months, there are plans afoot to utilize the yacht during the winter months too, in the slightly warmer waters of the Canary Islands and North Africa. That way, full use could be made of this lovely vessel. I find it remarkable and fascinating to look back and see just how wonderfully the Lord brought Release and *Genevieve* together.

How it all began

A bright Sunday morning in July 1997 found me in London. I was there with some friends of mine, and we decided to visit Holy Trinity Church in Brompton, which is just opposite the famous department store Harrods and is the church where the highly successful Alpha courses were first run. I had only ever been there once before and was looking forward to paying a second visit, as it seemed to be on the cutting edge of what God was doing at that time. Although I went along willingly, however, there were other things crowding my mind. Bob had only left three weeks earlier, and I was still trying to come to terms with all that was going on in my life. The difficulties I was experiencing made me more aware of the heartache being endured by other people who maybe did not know God in an intimate way. I knew that God loved everyone and was just longing to break through into each life, especially those going through trials, not only to walk with them through the bad times but also to develop and mature their characters.

We found a place where we could all sit together, and as I made myself comfortable I found a leather-bound Bible lying at the back of the seat. I guess it must have been left behind by the last person to sit there. As I picked it up, it fell open at Isaiah 61. I began to read what was before me, even though the service had just started. This is what I read:

> The Spirit of the Lord GOD is upon me, because the LORD has anointed me to bring good tidings to the afflicted; he has sent me to bind up the broken-hearted, to proclaim liberty to the captives, and the opening of the prison to those who are bound; to proclaim the year of the LORD's favour, and the day of vengeance of our God; to comfort all who mourn; to grant to those who mourn in Zion – to give them a garland instead of ashes, the oil of gladness instead of mourning, the mantle of praise instead of a faint spirit; that they may be called oaks of righteousness, the planting of the LORD, that he may be glorified (vv. 1-3 NKJV).

The words that I was reading just seemed to capture my frame of mind at that moment, knowing as I did that God is powerful enough to touch all who seek Him out and give their troubles to Him.

The rest of the congregation started to sing, and after a few moments I realized they were singing exactly the same words as I was reading! I was amazed. The Bible I was reading from did not belong to me, and I cannot remember ever picking up someone else's Bible before. It was not as though it was even a favourite passage of mine. Yet it was totally applicable to how I was feeling, and now it was being backed up by the chorus that the rest of the congregation started to sing. Thinking about it later, I knew that the Bible could have fallen open at any page – but it was that specific one at that specific time. I enjoyed the rest of the service, but do not remember a great deal of what was said. In my mind, I kept going over what I had read, wondering what implications the words from Isaiah had for me.

The story does not end there. Curiously enough, when the yacht *Genevieve* was passed to us by Tony Turner one year later, the text from Luke 4:18 that God had laid on his heart was read out as he handed the yacht over to us. The words read exactly the same as those in the first few verses of Isaiah 61.

Some might think that this was some kind of bizarre coincidence, but I sincerely believe that God had orchestrated the whole thing. I had felt for some time that there was a definite need for some sort of ministry centre which would be totally Bible based and would help people to find their divine purpose, enabling them to walk in liberty, but I did not at that time have the faintest idea what to do or how to go about it. I felt that the centre would need to have premises of its own, and pictured in my mind's eye the building being close to where I was living. Although I had a large house, I was not at all convinced that it should be used for that purpose, however.

Gradually, as the ideas began to form in my mind and the vision began to gel, I became confident enough to share my hopes and dreams with those I trusted. Other than that, I did nothing, apart from taking the matter to God.

Early the next year, around March, as I was driving down the road very near to where I live I passed an old Victorian building on my left, just as I had countless times before. Called Oakwood Court, it had stood empty and abandoned for many years, until 1996 when it was bought by a company for use as offices. They completely renovated the inside, stayed two years, and then put it on the market once again. Outside the building looked just the same as it always had. To the passer-by there was no indication at all of the work that had taken place inside. Seeing the 'For Sale' sign, however, I suddenly started to think about it as a possible location for the ministry centre. It was just one minute's walk from my home, and was in every sense ideally situated.

Arley is a mining village and Oakwood Court had originally belonged to the coal mine, which had closed before we moved to the village. The building was known as the 'Old Mine Rescue', but interestingly was normally referred to as 'The Rescue Centre', housing as it did at one time the apparatus used when miners were trapped underground in the shaft.

I made a mental note of the telephone number from the 'For Sale' sign and when I got home I rang the estate agents, wondering how much the asking price would be. I was told that it was in the final stages of being sold, and that they were unable to disclose how much the new owner had paid for it. I decided not to give my name: I was well known in the area, and did not want people knowing at that time that I might have been involved in the purchase of the building. I felt it curious, however, that they would not let me have even the basic details of the property, and wondered if things would be different if they got the same enquiry from a man. I rang Ralph, who worked at the church at the time as the administrator, and asked if he would be willing to give the agents a ring. The response to him was exactly the same. In spite of all this, however, I still felt that the building would be ideal, and could not get the premises out of my mind.

To my amazement a little while later, I became aware that the building was hitting the headlines in the local press. Apparently, the group that were purchasing the property wanted to change its use to school premises, so that underprivileged children could be taught there. It was alleged by some people, however, that similar schools in other neighbourhoods had a bad name, and that some of the pupils had caused disturbances in the villages in which they were located. How much of this was true, and how much of it was hearsay, I did not know and quite frankly I was not too interested. What did concern me was that the paper carrying the story also stated that a local Arley woman was leading a campaign to try to stop the group from occupying the school. It had nothing to do with me, but I did not want anyone to put two and two together and get six, thinking that because I had expressed a previous interest in the building I was involved in some way in stopping this group from carrying out their plans.

I therefore opted to keep quiet and did not mention it again. Several weeks passed, but in spite of the campaign and the petition that had been signed by many in the village, we heard on the grapevine that the local authority had granted the necessary permission for change of use to school premises. Everything seemed to come to an end for us as far as Oakwood Court was concerned. We heard nothing more for almost two months, and assumed that the sale was completed and the new group were about to take possession. Then, out of the blue, I received that all-important phone call from Ralph, moments after I had heard the Lord speak to me through Benny Hinn, and the whole project had new life breathed into it.

Although I had lived in the village for some 20 years, I had never set foot in the building that I had passed so often. When we eventually got to look around it, the property was much bigger than we had at first thought and the interior far surpassed all our expectations. It seemed tailor-made for the plans we had in mind. Set in three and a half acres of oak woodland, it had good office space, a room ideally suited for lectures, a board room, kitchen and dining facilities, and en-suite sleeping accommodation for over a dozen people. As I walked round, I could hardly believe that this was the same old building I had seen almost every day for the last two decades – just down the road from my house, and just a few miles from the convenient Midlands motorway network. I now began to understand why that other company had bought and refurbished it. They had carried out major renovations before they moved in, which would certainly have proved very costly and time consuming. What they had done, in effect, was to get the place ready for us to move into! Way before we even knew we would need a building, God was getting one ready for us. The more I think about that, the more I realize what an awesome God we serve.

Jesus never fails

After every sunset comes a sunrise and after every winter, without fail, comes a springtime. The faithfulness of God has always held me in awe. His eternal, unfailing love is beyond fathoming. He has never failed me and I know He never will, because He is the same yesterday and today and forever. My whole life has been blessed and filled with so many good things. They are the things upon which I now choose to dwell. I most certainly could never have planned the things that have happened to me in the last few years. It took a mastermind to do that, and I thank God every day for the way that He has led me to pastures that are lush and plenteous. He is a very dear and trusted friend, one who not only gives us what we need but who also knows and loves us so much that He desires to bestow upon us much more than we could ever dream. His supply is abundant and continuous. I know that He will never desert or reject me. He is for me, not against me.

We must constantly feed upon the Word of God so that we can stay strong and not falter or give way under the pressures of life. It cannot fail to make a difference. I can only tell you the things that have worked for me, but I know that they will work for you too. These are not formulas or systems that work for some and not for others. The principles and laws in the Bible, tried and tested by many, cannot fail to work for you if you cease looking to your own understanding and choose to trust and believe God and take Him at His Word. He will most definitely bring you safely through unscathed, if you are willing to do things in the way God, in his infinite wisdom, designed and lovingly planned. Instead of becoming bitter, you can become better – emotionally, physically, mentally and spiritually – even after the most devastating of experiences, even after a distressing and painful divorce.

I still wholeheartedly believe that any marriage, however bad or unhappy it has been, can be renewed and rejuvenated. I most certainly do not believe that there is such a thing as an 'irretrievable breakdown' with God. Absolutely any circumstances can be turned around by the power of the cross of Jesus, if both parties choose to allow God to do His work. Jesus' first miracle was turning unremarkable, everyday water into sparkling, delicious and refreshing wine. He is still in the business of turning the ordinary into the outstanding. No one on the face of this earth has to settle for less than the best, and the very best is what they will experience when they come into contact with the Risen Lord Jesus. The Bible tells us that Jesus kept the very best wine till last.

So, thank you for coming with me on my journey and staying until the very last page. It is so encouraging to know that, no matter how difficult or traumatic our past might have been, the moment we decide to obey God's Word and live according to His ways, our future immediately begins to change for the better. You can know without any doubt at all that, no matter how far down you feel you may have fallen, in God there is a glorious hope and a future. His arms are definitely long enough and strong enough to pull you out of the deepest and most foulest of pits.

Jeremiah was a prophet to the people of Israel at one of their lowest points, during the time when they were taken as slaves to a foreign land. Yet Jeremiah spoke a word of comfort into their seemingly impossible situation which gave them an undeniable hope for the future and made their present appalling circumstances much easier to bear. This is what God said through the mouth of Jeremiah to that crushed and defeated people: 'For I know the thoughts that I think toward you, says the LORD, thoughts of peace and not of evil, to give you a future and a hope' (Jeremiah 29:11 NKJV).

Thoughts of peace and not of evil, to give you a future and a hope. That is what the Lord has graciously given me. Another translation of the same verse (the Contemporary English Version) says, 'I will bless you with a future filled with hope.' It is a promise that you too can claim, whatever circumstances you happen to find yourself in, as you choose to put your whole trust in the all-wise God.

I know, without a doubt, that I have been sustained and brought through my time of trial by a much greater source of love, far above that of any spouse. As Paul the apostle so rightly said, our sorrows and afflictions can be regarded as mere stepping stones to even greater things. You can rest assured that God will never forsake you or abandon you. He is your rock and your fortress and 'a very present help in time of trouble'. The glorious truth is that He will be with you every inch of every journey in life, however difficult. He will never disappoint you or let you down, and He has a wonderful future planned for you – of that you can be absolutely sure.

Those wanting to know more about
Release Foundation can access the website at
www.releasefoundation.com

We want to hear from you. Please send your comments about
this book to us in care of the address below. Thank you.

ZONDERVAN™

GRAND RAPIDS, MICHIGAN 49530

WWW.ZONDERVAN.COM